MURD



# The SECRETS of SUMS

Kjartan
Poskitt

SCHOLASTIC

www.murderousmaths.co.uk

Scholastic Children's Books,
Euston House, 24 Eversholt Street,
London NW1 1DB, UK

A division of Scholastic Ltd
London ~ New York ~ Toronto ~ Sydney ~ Auckland
Mexico City ~ New Delhi ~ Hong Kong

Published by Scholastic Ltd, 2014

Some of the material in this book has previously been published in *Murderous Maths: The Mean and Vulgar Bits* (2000) and *Murderous Maths: Awesome Arithetricks* (1999)



ISBN 9788184776782



Printed at Ram Printograph, Delhi

Rreprinted by Scholastic India Pvt. Ltd., December 2015 Feb 2016

# CONTENTS



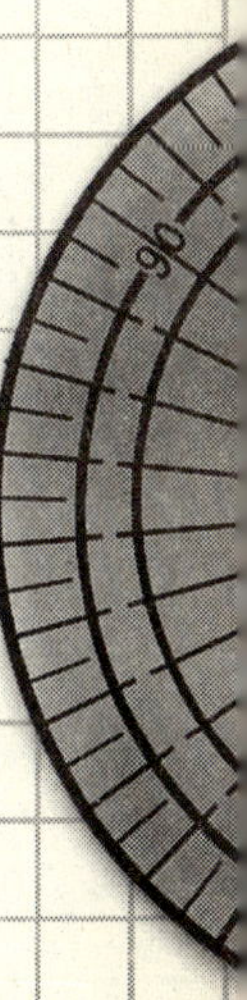

**KJARTAN POSKITT's** first jobs included playing pianos very loudly, presenting children's tv, inventing puzzles and writing pantomimes. Maths was his best subject at school, because it was the only one that didn't need good spelling and handwriting. As well as 30 maths books, he has written books about space, magic, codes and pants, and he also writes the Agatha Parrot and Borgon the Axeboy books. His favourite number is 12,988,816 because that's how many ways you can put 32 dominoes on a chessboard (although he didn't count them himself). If he wasn't an author he would like to have been a sound effects man. He has two old pinball tables, seven guitars and lots of dangerous old music synthesisers and he plays all of them... badly!

# WHY DO WE NEED THE SECRETS OF SUMS?

What do you like doing?

Sport? Cooking? Computer games? Music? Making models of large buildings from matchsticks? *Kissing*...???

Whatever it is, you'll never be an expert straight away. Even with kissing, you have to start at the bottom.

Maths is the same. Maybe one day you'll be clever enough to fly your own space rocket or build a skyscraper or maybe you'll invent an amazing new number that nobody else has thought of. WAHEY! But before you do that, you still have to start at the bottom and learn the basic stuff. We call it *The Secrets of Sums.*

It all starts with counting 1-2-3, then we move on to adding and multiplying and generally squidging numbers about, and then your brain will be all loaded up and ready to take over the universe.

Oh look! Somebody just sent us a letter...

Honestly! What a silly question.

If you only ever use a calculator, then you'll never be sure what's going on, because you're relying on a machine to do it all for you. It's a bit like if you wanted to be an artist, you have to start off doing nice simple pictures like this...

... but then you might end painting pictures that are worth millions!

However, that's never going to happen if you say this...

We all need sums for everything. If you're going on a trip you need to know how far it is, how long it will take and how many sandwiches you need to pack. If you become a sports star or a film star or a pop star, you need to know you're getting the right wages!

Even if you just go shopping, you need to know how much to pay and what change you should get. When it comes to working it out, the best person to trust is yourself.

So what are you waiting for? There's a whole world of tricks, games, fun and excitement waiting for you so long as you know the secrets of sums!

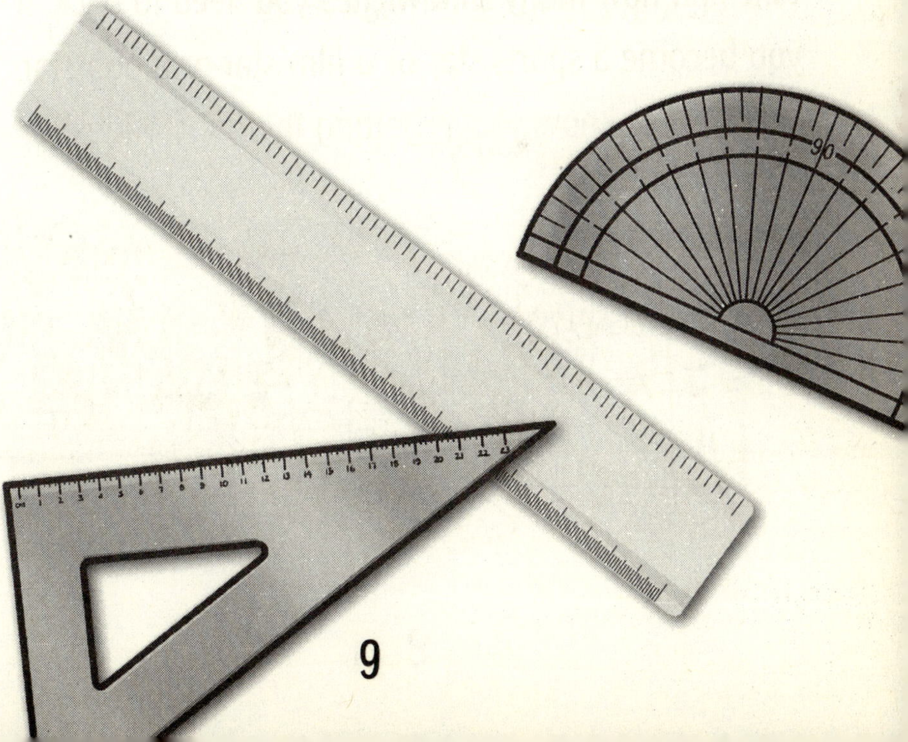

# BACK TO THE SANDPIT

Did you ever play in a sandpit when you were tiny? Do you wish that sandpit was a lesson at school, and when you get older you could do sandpit exams instead of worrying about sums?

Actually, it turns out that sums get everywhere, even into the sandpit. Look at this:

This is simple enough, so long as you know what "3" means, but there are some very clever people who can't decide what it is!

## Pure mathematicians – brilliant or bonkers?

As you probably know, scientists have found out that everything is made up of tiny atoms. That's why they spend a lot of time studying atoms to see what they are made of.

There are also people called *pure mathematicians* who worry about what numbers are. These people look quite normal, they get up and eat their cornflakes, but then they sit in an office all day and wonder "what is 3?"

If ever you meet some pure mathematicians, try asking them what number comes before one? It can drive them nuts.

Anyway, let's get back to the sandpit.

Imagine you are toddling up to have a turn, but there are three people already in it. How did you know? Because you managed to count 1-2-3 even if you did have a bit of dribble going down your chin.

Here's the clever bit. When you learnt to count, you started saying one, two, three in order, and then practised going up to higher numbers. But how high did you go? Let's see...

Suppose there are 35 kids in the sandpit, and four more come in. How many kids are in the sandpit now?

Easy! You start at 35 and count up one number for each extra kid that comes in: 36, 37, 38, 39.

But you never learnt to count all the numbers right up to 39 did you? Of course not, because your clever little brain realised that counting is just a set of tiny sums. You just add on one every time.

Even if there were 29,846,758 kids in the sandpit and four more came to join them, you wouldn't be worried.

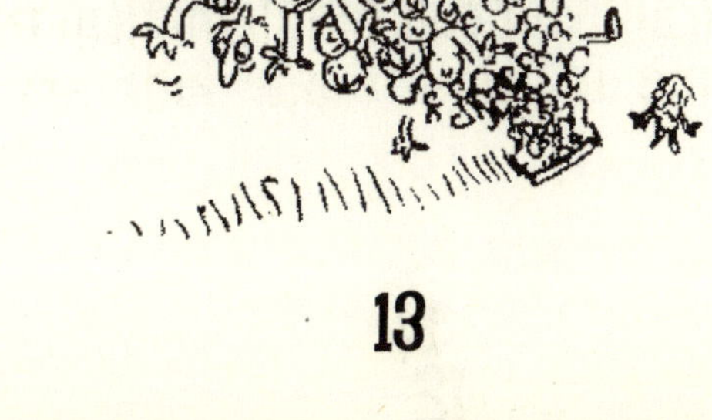

All you do is add on one for each kid that comes in so you get to 29,846,762. Now be honest, did anybody ever tell you about counting by adding one at a time? No? In that case you must have worked out this little trick all by yourself! Who's a little clever pants then?

Before we move on to some serious sums, you'll be wondering how counting can be murderous – after all this is supposed to be a book about murderous maths. Right then, picture the scene:

Your alarm clock has just gone off. "Tra-lah" you sing as you jump out of bed, but just as you are reaching for a sock, it twitches on the floor.

"Har har!" comes an evil voice from the top of the wardrobe. It's your arch enemy Professor Fiendish with a diabolically difficult mathematical trap.

"Har har!" he scowls again. "I've shoved thirteen deadly poisonous scorpions into your sock! What are you going to do about that then?"

Casually you tip the sock upside down and give it a flick. A bunch of little bodies clatter onto the floor and scurry away. You count them up and get twelve.

"Put it on then," sneers the professor.

"Not yet!" you say.

With a final flick you ping the thirteenth scorpion up at the professor.

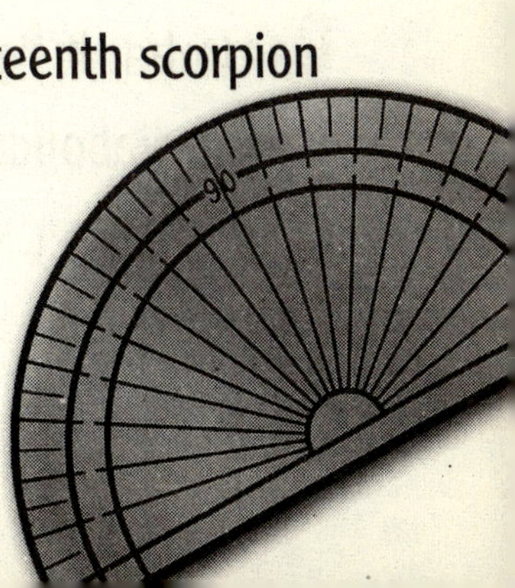

"Argh!" he wails as the scorpion stings the professor's warty nose.

"Your plan was brilliant, Fiendish," you say as you pull your socks on. "You just made one tiny mistake. You didn't count on me being able to count."

So there you are. Even counting can be murderous. Let's move on, shall we?

## Odd numbers

These are numbers that are not even. Gosh! What are even numbers then?

## Even numbers

These are numbers that are not odd. There, that was helpful wasn't it?

Even numbers are helpful if you're looking round a cinema showing a soppy love film. Everybody in the audience will be madly kissing each other, but how many people are there? In the dark all you can see are pairs of people huddled together, so you count them in TWOS!

What you do is walk up and down the rows carrying a very full beaker of ice-cold orange juice trying VERY HARD not to spill it on anybody. As you squeeze past each couple you count like this: 2-4-6...

So long as everybody is kissing another person, you will find there is an EVEN number of people. Even numbers always end in 2,4,6,8 or 0. (So 44, 210 and 38,937,856 are all even numbers.)

But when you finish counting the twos, you see Pongo McWhiffy sitting by all himself. Aw, poor Pongo! You'll have to add an extra one to your even number. This will give you an ODD number. Odd numbers always end in 1,3,5,7 or 9.

But then the lovely Veronica Gumfloss comes in. We have to add another one to our odd number of people, and that makes an even number again.

Odd, isn't it? And if you add another one to the even number it goes odd again which is even odder.

## Counting magic trick!

This extremely simple trick will catch out almost anybody. Ask your victim if he or she can count. The answer is bound to be yes, so then ask:

"Quick – what number comes next: nine thousand and ninety six, nine thousand and ninety seven, nine thousand and ninety eight, nine thousand and ninety nine...?"

Try it out on yourself first, in fact do it right now. What number do you think comes next?

If you said "ten thousand," write the numbers out in sequence and see what the right answer really is! (Remember – the first number is NOT nine thousand nine hundred and ninety six!)

## What is the difference between a number and a digit?

There are ten different digits and they are:

**1 2 3 4 5 6 7 8 9 0**.

You put digits together to make a number, just like you put letters together to make a word.

The word *bottigrub* is only one word but it has nine letters. (It also has 12 legs, 8 eyes and sharp teeth –YUK!)

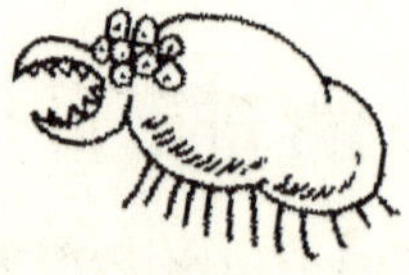

The number "4789" is only one number but it has four digits.

Some numbers only have one digit – for instance, how many eyes does this bellybug have?

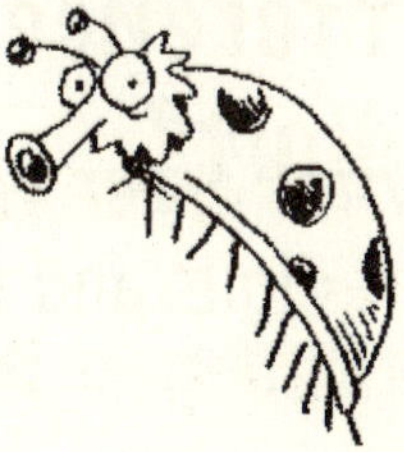

The answer is 2, which is both a digit and the number we need. It's clever stuff, isn't it?

# AWFUL ADDING

Here's the first secret of adding:

***It doesn't matter what order you add things in.***

Suppose you were sitting in the bath with four elephants, and two more elephants jumped in – you would end up in the bath with six elephants. This also works the other way round. If you start with two elephants then four more jump in, once again you'd end up with six elephants. In other words 4+2 is the same as 2+4 and they both come to 6.

(One of the great things about murderous maths is that you can always try these experiments out yourself. You'll find this one works perfectly, your only problem might be in finding out which elephant is sitting on the soap.)

Here's the second secret of adding:

***You can only add things that are the same.***

Let's say you have eight little dogs and you put them in a cage with four crocodiles. What have you got?

- Twelve crocodiles?
- Twelve dogs?
- A mixture of crocodiles and dogs? (*this is the right answer if you didn't know.)
- Four very happy burping crocodiles who are ready for a quiet snooze?

You get the point.

Even if you are just adding up numbers, make sure you only add things that are the same. Look at this:

$$324+61$$

The problem is that you have added things that are not the same. Ooh, naughty!

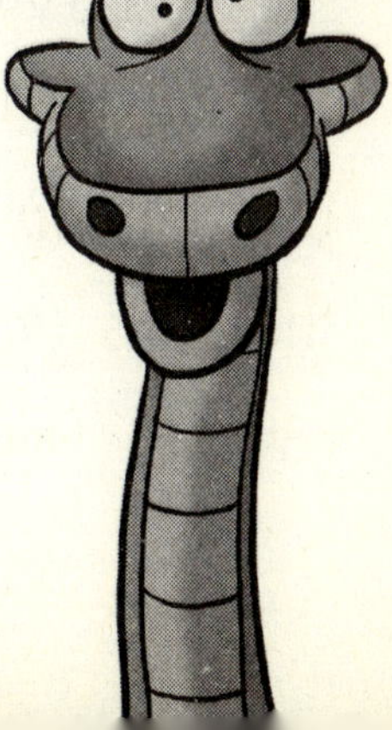

Remember this:

### *Each digit in a number means something different*

When you have 324, that's 3 hundreds, 2 tens and 4 units. 61 is 6 tens and 1 unit. You can only add hundreds to hundreds, tens to tens and units to units!

Here's how we usually write this sum down:

| | hundreds ↓ | tens ↓ | units ↓ |
|---|---|---|---|
| | 3 | 2 | 4 |
| + | | 6 | 1 |
| = | | | |

You don't have to write "hundreds, tens and units" over the top. That's just to show you how we've put the units (4 and 1), the tens (2 and 6), and the hundreds (3) into different columns so they don't get mixed up.

Here comes the next secret of happy adding:

***Always start with the units!***

You get 4+1 = 5 so you write 5 underneath in the answer box. Then you add up the tens so you get 2+6 = 8, and you put the 8 in the answer box. The 3 hundreds don't have any other hundreds to add to, so they just go straight into the answer box, and you get…

$$\begin{array}{rr} & 324 \\ + & 61 \\ \hline = & 385 \end{array}$$

That wasn't too bad, was it?

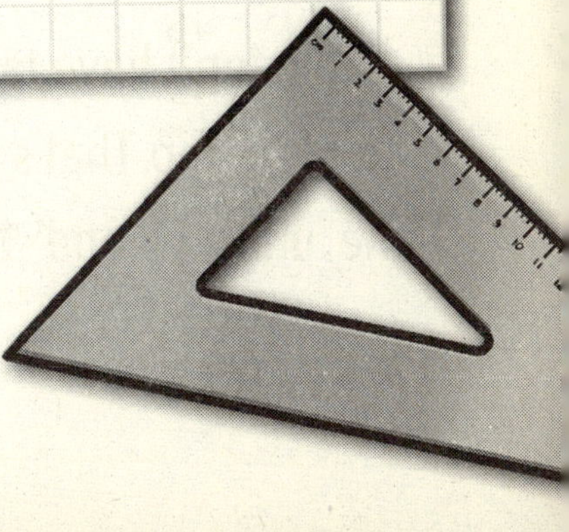

Oh no! It's Professor Fiendish again with an EVIL sum for us to try!

Gosh, he wants us to add three numbers all together at once... AND we're about to get an extra thrill that we haven't seen yet!

First we'll write the numbers out like this:

```
    417
+    48
+   189
   ____
=
   ____
```

← A thrilling gap

Because of this extra thrill, we need to leave a gap under the answer line. As usual we'll start by adding up the units:

7+8+9 comes to 24.

Gosh, how thrilling! In our answer 24, we have 4 units – and also 2 tens! We write down the 4 units in the answer box, but what do we do with the 2 tens? It's no good just hoping that they'll go away, so we "carry them over" into the tens column.

```
    417
+    48
+   189
  -----
=     4
  -----
     2
```

← Filling the thrilling gap with "carried over" numbers

We've written the 2 tens as a little "2" in the thrilling gap underneath the tens column. We now add up all the tens, *including the 2 tens we just carried over!* We get 1+4+8+2, which comes to 15. Just as we did with the units, we write down the 5 tens in the answer box, but we carry over the 10 tens (which makes 1 hundred) by putting a little "1" in the hundreds place in the thrilling gap.

$$\begin{array}{lr} & 417 \\ + & 48 \\ + & 189 \\ \hline = & 54 \\ \hline & {\scriptstyle 1\ 2} \end{array}$$

← **Still filling the thrilling gap.**

We now add up the hundreds (including the one we carried over) and get 4+1+1 which makes 6.

$$\begin{array}{rr} & 417 \\ + & 48 \\ + & 189 \\ \hline = & 654 \\ \hline & \scriptstyle \not{1}\,\not{2}\ \ \end{array}$$

← Once you've got the answer, you can cross off the carried-over numbers if you like.

There – we've finished! Relax, take a shower and have a cup of tea. You deserve it.

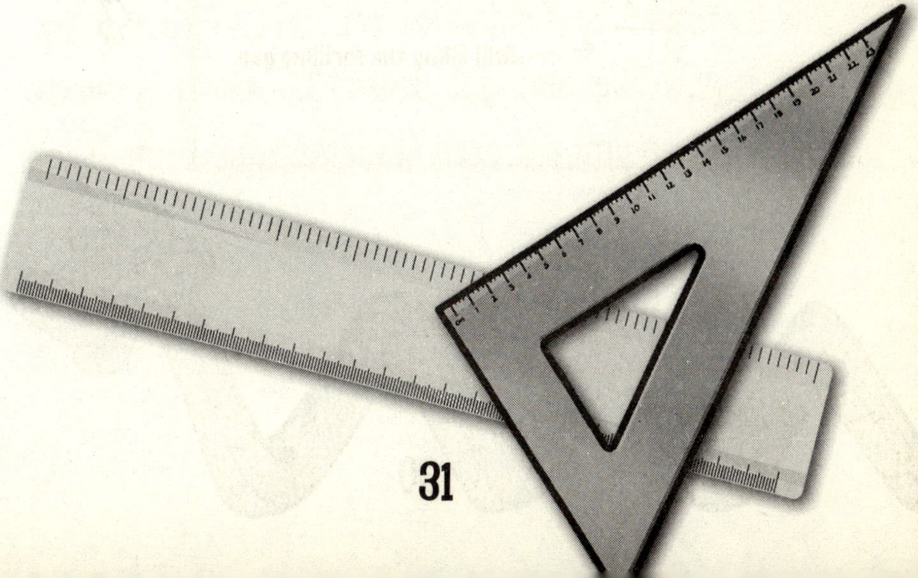

## Bigger numbers

So far we've only seen units, tens and hundreds, but numbers can be as long as you like. If you have the number 5,894,732, this is what each digit is worth:

| 5 | 8 | 9 | 4 | 7 | 3 | 2 |
|---|---|---|---|---|---|---|
| millions | 100,000s | 10,000s | 1,000s | 100s | 10s | units |

(The commas are just there to show you where the thousands and millions start. You can leave them out if you like and get 5894732 which is more useful when you are getting on with the sums.)

## Adding money

When you add up money, it's even more important to write out your numbers in the right place. Suppose you've been shopping and want to add up what you've spent. It might look like this:

```
£ 3.50
    28p
£11.35
    80p
```

Here you can see single pennies are in a column, "tens" of pennies are in a column, so are single pounds and "tens" of pounds.

## Other ways of saying "adding"

Because adding things up is so common, there are lots of different ways of saying it.

- You can ADD UP a set of numbers
- You can get the TOTAL of a set of numbers.
- You can find the SUM of a set of numbers.

# SICKLY SUBTRACTING

Subtracting is also called *taking-away* and it has a very simple little sign -. This is called the *minus* sign and it looks quite harmless until you get your magnifying glass out!

Eeek! But don't worry, we'll soon have this little beast under control.

If a number has a minus sign in front of it, it's called a negative number and you have to take it away. Here's a game to give you a bit of practise at adding and subtracting.

# Frazzle or fish food?

What you need:
A 6-sided die
A coin
A counter for each player

How to play:
Players start with their counters on 0, beside the boat.
Players take turns to toss the coin and throw the die.

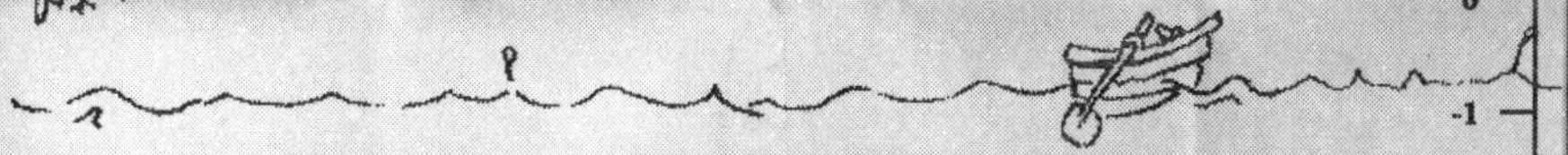

If the coin lands HEADS, you move up the same number of places as the number on the die. If the coin lands TAILS, you move down the number of places on the die. BUT if you get a SIX, ignore the coin and go back to the boat.
If you hit the sun you are frazzled to bits!
If you reach the shark, you get eaten!
The last person left alive is the winner.
(If the coin is HEADS, this makes the number on the die + or *positive*. If the coin is TAILS then the number is – or *negative*. Positive and negative numbers move in opposite ways, and can cancel each other out.)

## Really simple subtracting

Back in the sandpit there are now 51 kids. Suddenly some giant boney hands come out of the sand and pull three of them underground to turn them into zombies. How many kids are left?

We can write the sum like this 51-3 = ? and to work it out, we just count down one number for each person that has gone. We start at 51 then count down three places: 50-49-48 and so 48 is the answer.

Counting down is only useful when you're taking away a small number. What if we had 81 kids in the sandpit and 57 of them got turned into zombies? How many kids would be left?

The sum looks like this 81-57 = ?

This is too much to count down, especially if you were using your fingers. You would have to take your socks off and use your toes too AND you'd have to borrow somebody else's fingers and toes as well.

This can get a bit embarrassing, so instead we'll work out the answer with a nice little trick. Instead of subtracting, we're going to add!

We start with 57 and see what we need to add on to make 81. We can do this in easy bits.

First we say that 57+3 = 60

Here we've added 3.

Then say 60+20 = 80

Now we've added 20 more.

Finally we say 80+1 = 81.

We've added another 1.

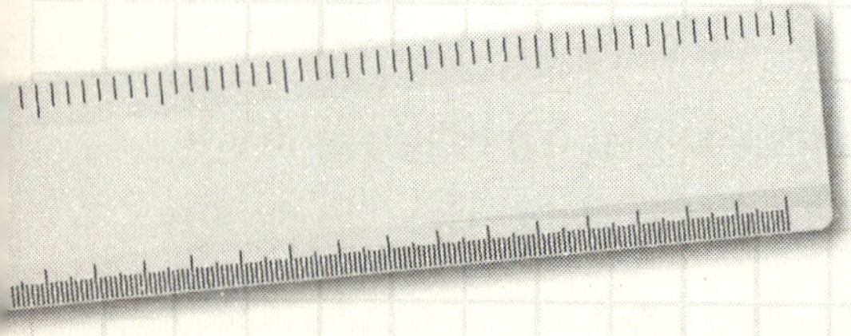

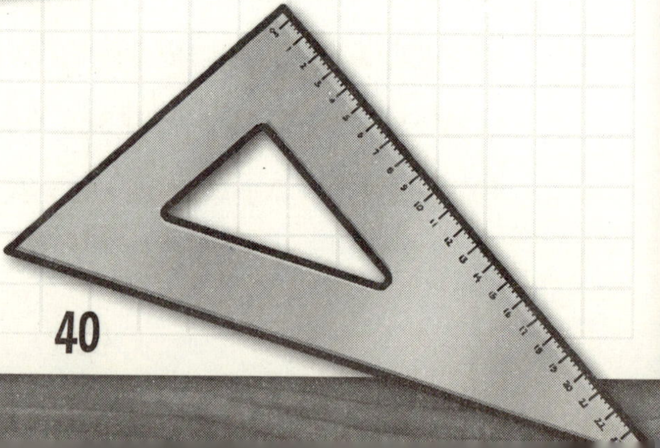

So how much did we add on altogether? It was 3+20+1 which altogether makes 24. That's the answer! 81-57 = 24. With a bit of practise, you should be able to do sums like this in your head, as long as the zombies aren't attacking you.

## Serious subtracting

Bigger subtractions are like bigger additions for two reasons:

- you can only take away things that are the same, so you can only take units from units and you can only take tens from tens and so on.
- you always start with the units.

How about this: 459-312 = ?

If you write out the numbers neatly, the answer should just fall in the right place!

$$\begin{array}{r} 459 \\ -\ 312 \\ \hline =\ 147 \\ \hline \end{array}$$

We always take the bottom number from the top one, so starting with the units we get 9-2 = 7. Then we do the tens and get 5-1 = 4 and finally the hundreds, 4-3 = 1.

That was too easy, so let's crack another…

```
  372
-  45
=____
```

It's looks simple, but when we start with the units we get 2-5 = -3. Oh dear! That's a *minus* 3, and we can't just ignore the naughty little minus sign. We need to get some extra units from somewhere!

• There's a 7 in the tens column which is worth 70, so we take 10 from that. This leaves 60, so we cross out the 7 and replace it with a 6.

• Next we add this extra 10 to the 2 in the units column to make 12.

• Now we can take away our 5 from the 12. We get 12-5 = 7.

• We've done the units, so it's time to look at the tens. We've got 6 tens left on the top and we need to take away 4, so 6-4 = 2. We write this in the answer.

• As there are no hundreds to take away, we just bring down the 3 to give the answer 327.

Invite your friends for a cup of tea.

When people do these sums, they normally end up looking like this:

Take a ten from here ↘ and put it here ↙

$$
\begin{array}{cccc}
 & 3 & \not{7}^{6} & {}^{1}2 \\
- & & 4 & 5 \\
\hline
= & 3 & 2 & 7 \\
\hline
\end{array}
$$

You can see how the 7 has been changed into a 6, and then the extra 10 turns the 2 units into 12. After that the sum is easy!

## Check your change

Subtracting is very handy for checking your change in shops. This could be handy if the evil Gollarks from the planet Zog decide to attack us.

Don't worry. So long as everybody paints stars all over their house, then Earth will just blend in with the rest of the sky and the Gollarks will never find us.

Star paint costs £3.79 and you pay with a £5 note, so what change should you get?

| | | |
|---|---|---|
| | £5.00 | money you paid |
| - | £3.79 | cost of paint |
| = | £1.21 | the change you should get |

Remember to write the numbers directly above each other just like in addition.

If you want to check your sum, just add the bottom two numbers together and see if you get the top one. In this case you get £1.21+£3.79 and you'll find it comes to £5. Oh, and you needn't worry about the Gollarks…

## Other names for subtractions

Look at this sum:

$$15 - 9 = ?$$

There are lots of ways of describing it.

- You can "subtract" 9 from 15
- You can "take away" 9 from 15
- You can "reduce" 15 by 9
- You can find the "difference" of 15 and 9
- You could have 15 and "knock off" 9
- And of course it's also 15 "minus" 9

# A SECRET CODE!

You can use adding and subtracting to send coded messages! Before you start you have to write out your message, then swap each letter for a number. The simplest way to swap them is this:

| | | | | | | | | | | |
|---|---|---|---|---|---|---|---|---|---|---|
| A | B | C | D | E | F | G | H | I | J | K |
| 1 | 2 | 3 | 4 | 5 | 6 | 7 | 8 | 9 | 10 | 11 |
| L | M | N | O | P | Q | R | S | T | | |
| 12 | 13 | 14 | 15 | 16 | 17 | 18 | 19 | 20 | | |
| U | V | W | X | Y | Z | | | | | |
| 21 | 22 | 23 | 24 | 25 | 26 | | | | | |

Suppose you wanted to say "Hello Granny", it would come out like this:

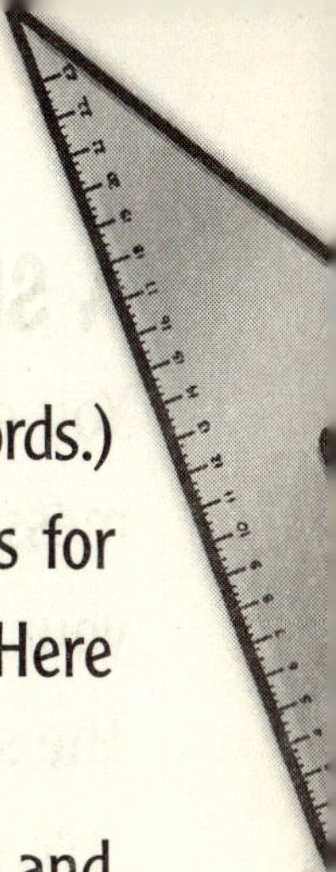

8 5 12 12 15 7 18 1 14 14 25

(Codes usually miss out the spaces between words.)

All we've done so far is swapped the letters for numbers, we haven't put it into code yet. Here comes the good bit!

To ENCODE your message you use adding and you also need a KEY number. This can be any number you like, but you should only tell it to your granny or whoever else the message is for. Let's say the key number for this message is 11. You write the key number in front of the message…

11 8 5 12 12 15 7 18 1 14 14 25

…then add up each number with the one that comes after it. So for this coded message you get 11+8 = 19, then 8+5 = 13, then 5+12 = 17 and so on. Here's the coded message all ready to send:

19 13 17 24 27 22 25 19 15 28 39

This is a very tough code to break if you don't know the key number!

To DECODE the message, your granny writes the key number under the first number of the coded message, then subtracts it. (In this case she'll get 19-11 = 8) She then takes the answer away from the second number (here she gets 13-8 = 5), and then she takes that answer away from the next number, and keeps going to the end.

| | | | | | | | | | | | |
|---|---|---|---|---|---|---|---|---|---|---|---|
| | 19 | 13 | 17 | 24 | 27 | 22 | 25 | 19 | 15 | 28 | 39 |
| - | 11 | 8 | 5 | 12 | | | | | | | |
| = | 8 | 5 | 12 | **and so on....** | | | | | | | |

The original message will appear along the bottom!

For extra security, you could have a system where the key number keeps changing, but make sure granny writes the numbers down somewhere!

Later in this book there is a joke that is SO RUDE that it had to be coded, otherwise all the people working in *Murderous Maths* bookshops would be arrested and given 5 years of geography homework. We've hidden the key number in a big sum, and we'll tell you how to find it when you get there!

## Even more good news

If you think that adding and subtracting is too easy to bother with, here's a brilliant fact:

***NEARLY EVERYTHING IN MATHS CAN BE DONE JUST BY ADDING AND SUBTRACTING***

It's true, but it does mean that a lot of sums would take a very long time. That's why it's worth reading the rest of this book because everything else is a SHORT CUT. For instance, you could work this horrid sum out purely by adding and subtracting:

$235{,}894 \times 4{,}388 \div 974 =$

but it would take you months and drive you utterly potty. That's why it's worth getting your head round...

# THE TERRIBLE TABLES

Teachers try all sorts of wild and wonderful ways to make the times tables interesting. Here's how they did it in the old days:

And here are some of the ways they do it these days:

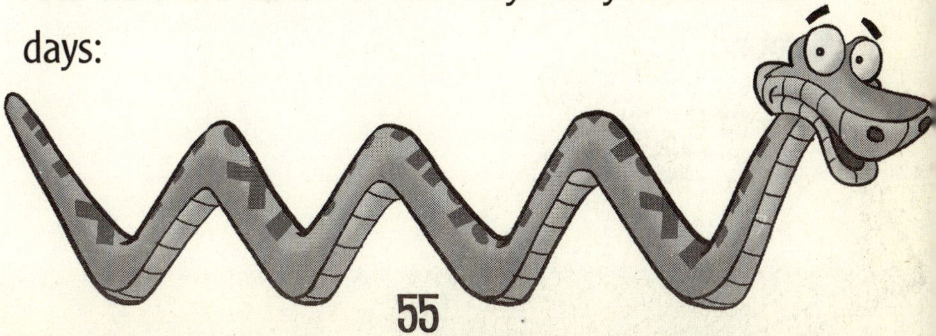

# Cutesy

# Musical

# Bribery

## Bonding

## Competition

## Hypnosis

## Sad

So what's the best way to learn the times tables? Let's fly across the universe and see how a highly advanced alien civilization do it...

## Do yourself a BIG favour!

Even if the times tables drive you mad, LEARN THEM.

Once you've done it, you'll remember them for ever, and it's like having a secret weapon in your head. The times tables help you with shopping, organizing, travelling, building, camping, eating bananas, choosing which trousers to wear... well maybe not all those things, but the point is, they make life so much easier!

Look at these six ladies. They eat nine cakes each, so how many cakes is that altogether?

• You could just add up six lots of nine cakes which is 9+9+9+9+9+9. It comes to 54 cakes, but it was a bit boring to do.

• Use your secret weapon – the times tables! 6×9 = 54. If you like you can do it the other way round: 9×6 = 54. It's a lot faster, isn't it?

That was multiplying. If you know the tables properly you can do the same sum backwards which is dividing.

There are six ladies charging at a pile of 54 cakes. How many can they each have? We could do the sum by subtracting:

Start with 54 cakes. Give each lady one cake, so that's six cakes less. How many cakes are left? 54-6 = 48. Give each lady a second cake, then see how many are left. 48-6 = 42. Now give each lady a third cake … OH BOY is this dull or what? We'll try something different.

If you know your tables, as soon as you see the number 54, a little bell will ring in your head.

Straight away you can say that the six ladies will get nine cakes each. As you can see, it's well worth knowing the times tables, so here they come!

# The terrible times tables

| | 1 | 2 | 3 | 4 | 5 | 6 | 7 | 8 | 9 | 10 |
|---|---|---|---|---|---|---|---|---|---|---|
| 01 | 1 | 2 | 3 | 4 | 5 | 6 | 7 | 8 | 9 | 10 |
| 02 | 2 | 4 | 6 | 8 | 10 | 12 | 14 | 16 | 18 | 20 |
| 03 | 3 | 6 | 9 | 12 | 15 | 18 | 21 | 24 | 27 | 30 |
| 04 | 4 | 8 | 12 | 16 | 20 | 24 | 28 | 32 | 36 | 40 |
| 05 | 5 | 10 | 15 | 20 | 25 | 30 | 35 | 40 | 45 | 50 |
| 06 | 6 | 12 | 18 | 24 | 30 | 36 | 42 | 48 | 54 | 60 |
| 07 | 7 | 14 | 21 | 28 | 35 | 42 | 49 | 56 | 63 | 70 |
| 08 | 8 | 16 | 24 | 32 | 40 | 48 | 56 | 64 | 72 | 80 |
| 09 | 9 | 18 | 27 | 36 | 45 | 54 | 63 | 72 | 81 | 90 |
| 10 | 10 | 20 | 30 | 40 | 50 | 60 | 70 | 80 | 90 | 100 |

If you pick any two numbers between 1 and 10, you can quickly find what they multiply to make. How about 6×8 ? Look along the "8" row and down the "6" column, and find the answer 48.

If you want to practise the tables, pick one of the numbers down the side, let's say "7". You then work along the row saying: "Seven times one is seven, seven times two is fourteen, seven times three is twenty one..." and keep going until you get to "seven times ten is seventy".

It's worth doing this a few times just to get the feel of it, but now we're going to make the numbers more interesting. To start with, we're going to get rid of most of them!

• Anything times by 1 gives the same answer. (So 4×1 = 4)

**That's so easy, we'll get rid of the 1 row and the 1 column.**

• Anything times by 10 just gets a 0 plonked on the end. (So 4×10 = 40. Easy peasy.)

**So we'll get rid of the 10 row and the 10 column.**

• Any multiplying sum is the same backwards as it is forwards, so 6×8 is the same as 8×6.

**This means that we can get rid of any sum that appears twice!**

Let's see what's left...

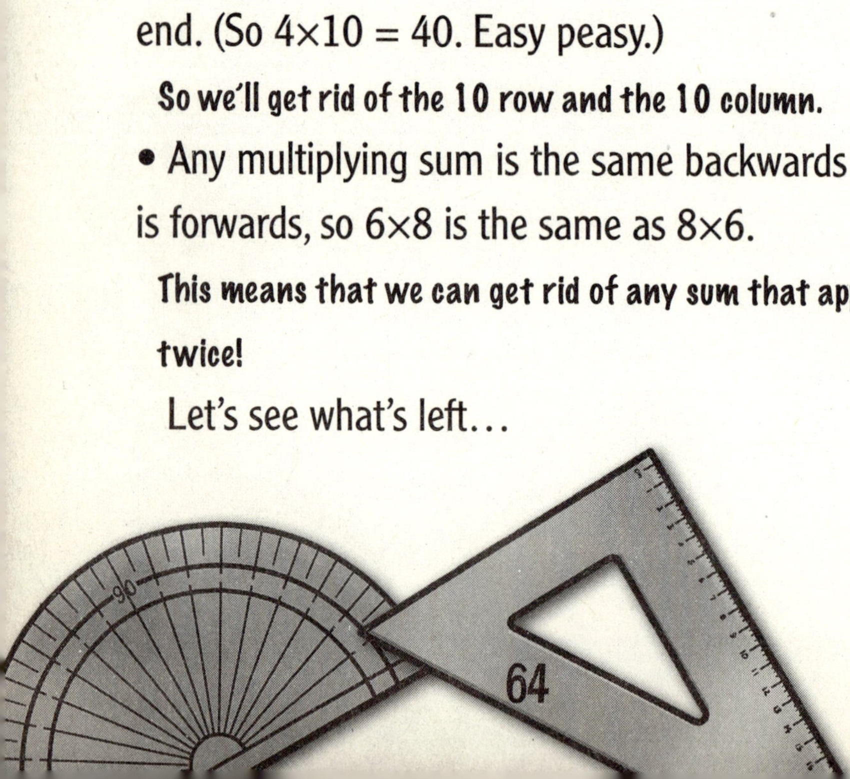

# The terribly interesting table!

| | 2 | 3 | 4 | 5 | 6 | 7 | 8 | 9 |
|---|---|---|---|---|---|---|---|---|
| 2 | 4 | | | | | | | |
| 3 | 6 | 9 | | | | | | |
| 4 | 8 | 12 | 16 | | | | | |
| 5 | 10 | 15 | 20 | 25 | | | | |
| 6 | 12 | 18 | 24 | 30 | 36 | | | |
| 7 | 14 | 21 | 28 | 35 | 42 | 49 | | |
| 8 | 16 | 24 | 32 | 40 | 48 | 56 | 64 | |
| 9 | 18 | 27 | 36 | 45 | 54 | 63 | 72 | 81 |

(YOU COULD RENT OUT THIS SPACE FOR ADVERTS)

That looks better, but there are still a lot of numbers left to learn. It's a bit like looking at a photo of a crowd, which is very boring...

...until you see that one person has two heads and another one is an alien and so on. As soon as a few people become interesting, then the whole photo is more fun.

It's the same with the numbers in the times tables. First of all, see if you can spot these two trick sums:

12 = 3×4 (See? The digits go 1-2-3-4)

56 = 7×8

Some numbers turn up twice in the middle. 16 is one of them because 2×8 = 16 and 4×4 = 16. There are four others, so can you find them? Here's a clue – these four are all in the 6 times table!

Can you find your own favourite numbers? If your house number is 32, the table says that's 8×4 (or 4×8 of course). Imagine sending yourself a postcard with this on it:

Another interesting number might be your birthday. Suppose it's the 15th of the month, you could tell everybody it's the 3×5 of the month. With a bit of luck they might get confused and give you presents on the 3rd, the 5th AND the 15th. Nice one!

The numbers coming down the sloping line (4, 9, 16 etc.) are handy because they are called SQUARES. Squares are what you get when you multiply a number by itself. For instance 9 is 3×3 which is only half as hard to remember.

Here's an odd trick. Pick any one of the squares. Move down one place and left one place. The number you get to is always one less! So if you start at 64 (which is 8×8), when you move down one and left one you get to 63 (which is 9×7).

Something else to do is colour in all the ODD

numbers. (That is, any numbers ending in 1,3,5,7 or 9). You'll see that a pattern appears.

By the time you've finished playing with these numbers, you'll feel like your head has been fitted with a calculator!

## Easy eleven and the twelve times trick

The tables from 1-10 are all you need to do any multiplying sums, but there are two more tables which can come in handy.

The 11 times table is rather good fun! It starts like this...

$1 \times 11 = 11$

$2 \times 11 = 22$

$3 \times 11 = 33$...

...and so on up to $9 \times 11 = 99$.

The fun part is when you multiply 11 by a two digit number. All you need to do is add the two digits up and put the answer in the middle! So for 12×11 you add up 1+2 which makes 3, then put it in the middle. The answer is 132!

We just need to be a bit careful multiplying 11 by bigger numbers. If we're inviting 79 football teams to a party, we'll need to know how many funny hats we need, so we work out 79×11.

We add 7+9 to get 16, but if we put 16 in the middle we get 7169, which is a LOT of hats! What we should do here is put the 6 in the middle, then add the 1 onto the 7, so we get $79 \times 11 = 869$.

The 12 times table is also handy because you often buy things in packets of 12, and older people talk about "dozens" of things, which means lots of twelves.

For the 12 times table, the secret is to add the 2 times table to the 10 times table! So you just multiply your number $\times$ 2, then add your number onto the tens column. If you wanted $7 \times 12$, you do $7 \times 2 = 14$, then add 7 to the tens to get 84.

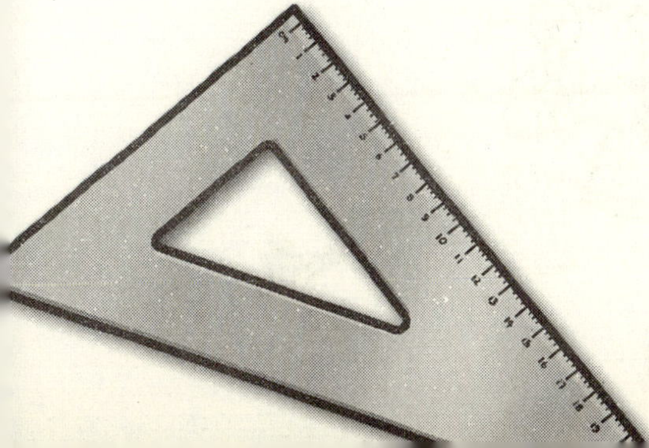

## Here's the whole thing:

| number | 1 | 2 | 3 | 4 | 5 | 6 | 7 | 8 | 9 | 10 | 11 | 12 |
|---|---|---|---|---|---|---|---|---|---|---|---|---|
| ×2 | 2 | 4 | 6 | 8 | 10 | 12 | 14 | 16 | 18 | 20 | 22 | 24 |
| ×10 | +10 | +20 | +30 | +40 | +50 | +60 | +70 | +80 | +90 | +100 | +110 | +120 |
| ×12 | =12 | =24 | =36 | =48 | =60 | =72 | =84 | =96 | =108 | =120 | =132 | =144 |

## Head stretchers

When you know the times tables, you'll find you can do some awesome sums in your head! How about this: 200×9,000?

Relax! Just work out $2 \times 9$, which you know from the tables is 18. You then count up all the zeros in the sum (here we've got five of them) and write them afterwards to get the answer 1,800,000. You'll see we've just put the commas in to make it look tidier.

Here's another: $800 \times 50{,}000 = 40{,}000{,}000$. This is because $8 \times 5 = 40$, and then you put another six zeros on, because that's how many there were in the original sum.

Oh gosh – it looks like you've found out about the tables just in time because this book has been sabotaged! Did you notice the black blob on the last page? That isn't normal ink, that's a knock-out sleeping potion and when you read the page you accidentally put your thumb on it. Although you haven't realised it, you are now FAST ASLEEP and about to face an utterly diabolical challenge...

## The morphing maze

"Where am I?" you groan as you open your eyes.

"Har har!" comes a voice. "This time you'll never beat me."

Oh no, it's Professor Fiendish again. You see that you are in a passage with a large number nine painted on the floor in front of you.

"What's that nine for?" you ask.

"You cannot pass over it without dividing yourself into the nine and morphing into another number," said the professor.

"What are you wittering on about?" you reply.

"Look!" he says triumphantly, and holds up a mirror.

Gosh! Your whole body has been replaced by a large number 1.

"To get down the passage you must divide yourself into the 9 and see what you turn into!" laughs the professor.

"So here I'm dividing nine by one, so I just get nine," you say as you step over the number.

ZAP! Your body morphs into a figure 9! This is pretty weird, even by the professor's standards. You see three other passages leading away, each with a number painted on the floor.

"You can only pass over numbers that you can divide exactly into," chuckles the professor. "And when you have passed over, you turn into the answer!"

You see a number 72 on the floor and step over it.

ZAP! Your body turns from a 9 into an 8. (You remember the tables and realize this is because

9×8 = 72.) You step back and ZAP your body becomes a 9 again.

There is an 81 which you step over. ZAP you become another 9. Of course – that's because 9×9 = 81. You step back and ZAP, you are still a nine.

Just round a corner you see a 64 which you try and step over. KERCHANGG! A massive metal spike shoots out of the floor and just misses you.

"Har har!" says the professor. "Nine won't go into 64, and that's why you can't pass over it."

"What's the point of all this?" you ask.

"The only way you can get your body back is to reach the bottle of antidote, but you'll only get there if you cross the numbers in this order!"

You see he is waving a piece of paper, but then a sudden breeze blows it away to another page in this book.

"Oops!" giggled the Professor. "Now you'll have to work out which way to go yourself, but I don't fancy your chances!"

Diabolical indeed! But maybe, just maybe, if you keep a cool head and use the tables you can get right through the morphing maze and reach the antidote!

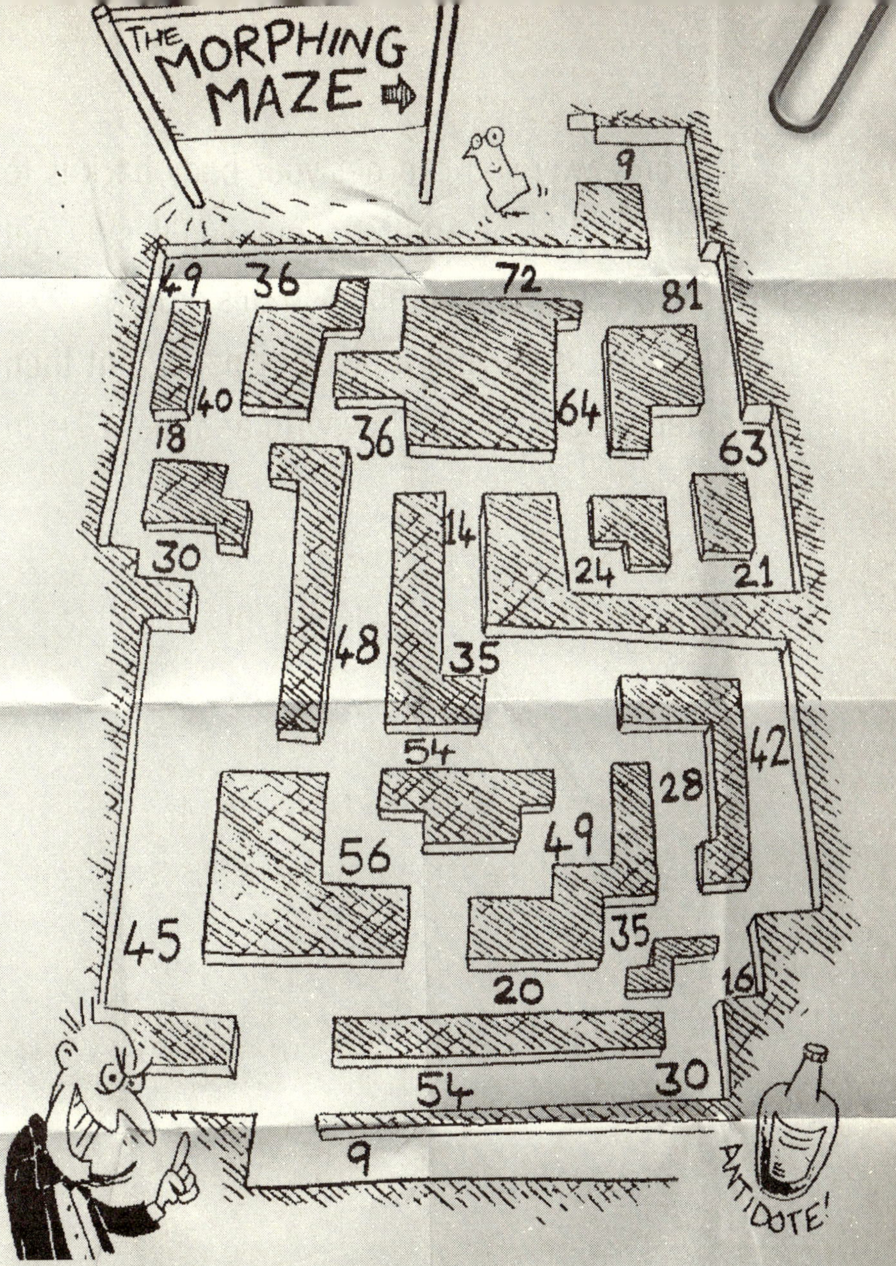


The answer is on page 132

# MAD MULTIPLYING

Once you know the tables, you'll find that multiplying bigger numbers is easy peasy. Look at this:

$$\begin{array}{r} 7 \\ \times\ 29 \\ \hline = \quad\ \ \\ \hline \end{array}$$

Before we start, here's a little helpful secret:

***With multiplying, it's usually easier to have the bigger number on the top.***

Luckily you're allowed to swap the numbers round when you're multiplying, so let's have this instead:

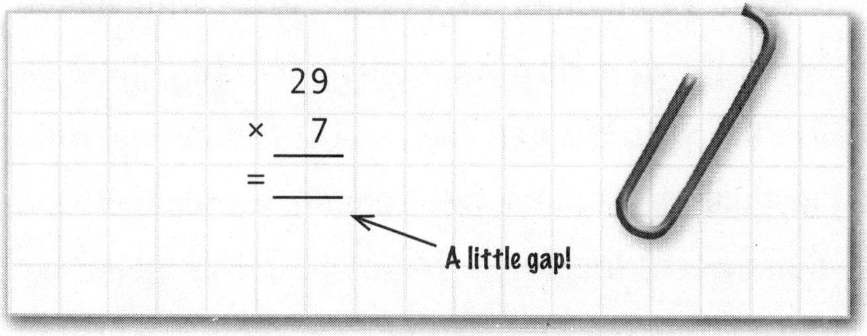


You'll see one of our little gaps has appeared too, which will come in handy.

Off we go then. All we do is take the lower number and multiply it by the upper number starting with the units. First do 7×9 which makes 63. This is the same as six tens and three units, so we write the 3 units down in the units place.

$$\begin{array}{r} 29 \\ \times \quad 7 \\ \hline = \quad 3 \\ \hline {\scriptstyle 6} \end{array}$$

We mustn't forget the six tens, so we write a little "6" in the gap. Now we multiply the 7 by the 2 on the top row. We get 2×7 = 14. Before we write anything down in the tens column, we see there are 6 more tens to add on. 14+6 = 20. This means we put a "0" in the tens column, and carry a 2 over to the hundreds. As there is nothing left on the top line to multiply, we can write the 2 in the answer box.

$$\begin{array}{r} 29 \\ \times \quad 7 \\ \hline = \; 203 \\ \hline {\scriptstyle 6} \end{array}$$

And that's it!

## A little short cut

Some multiplying sums have short cuts, and this is one of them!

Suppose you had 29 sheep. That would be the same as having 30 sheep, but with one sheep missing. It's the same with sevens. 29 sevens is the same as 30 sevens, but with one missing. Therefore to work this sum out, just do 30×7, which is 210, then take one seven away. You get 210-7 = 203.

You can use this trick whenever the big number ends in 9. If you have 79×6, that's the same as having 80 sixes, and then taking one away. You get 80×6 = 480, and then 480-6 = 474. With a bit of practise you can zap these in your head! Pretty cool, eh?

# A spot of trouble...

Phew! Thank goodness we were here, because this nurse needs some help from the heroes of *Murderous Maths*. (That's us.)

The numbers might look nasty but we're not scared. Let's get them organized into a sum:

| | | |
|---|---|---|
| | 12834 | total number of people |
| × | 217 | spots on each person |
| = | | total number of spots |

Here's the secret to sorting out massive sums like this:

***You can split big multiplications into lots of simple little sums, then add the answers all together***

To start with we get the smaller number and split it up into units, tens, hundreds and so on. Here we'll split the 217 into 200+10+7. All we need to do is multiply 12,834 by each of these bits then add the three answers up.

Yes please.

## Multiplying by hundreds

First, let's make sure we know how to multiply by 10:

***To multiply by any number by 10, you move it all one place to the left and then plonk an extra "0" on the end***

Multiplying by hundreds is just as easy:

***To multiply by any number by 100, you move it all two places to the left and then plonk "00" on the end***

Thanks. While it's cooling let's remember what we're working out. It's 12834×217.

First we multiply the 12834 by the 200, which is the same as multiplying by 2 and then using our "hundreds" trick of moving the answer along two places and putting "00" on the end.

$$\begin{array}{r} 12834 \\ \times \quad 200 \\ \hline = 2566800 \\ \hline \end{array}$$

Now we multiply by the 10 which is easy peasy:

$$\begin{array}{r} 12834 \\ \times \quad 10 \\ \hline = 128340 \\ \hline \end{array}$$

And finally we multiply by the "7":

$$\begin{array}{r} 12834 \\ \times \quad 7 \\ \hline = 89838 \\ \hline {\scriptstyle 1\,5\,2\,2} \end{array}$$

Now that we've done the little bits, we can add the three answers up.

CHOMP
CHOMP

$$\begin{array}{rl} 2566800 & \text{(This is 12834x200)} \\ +\quad 128340 & \text{(This is 12834x10)} \\ +\quad 89838 & \text{(This is 12834x7)} \\ \hline =\ 2784978 & \text{(And this is 12834x217)} \\ \hline \end{array}$$

And there's the final answer.

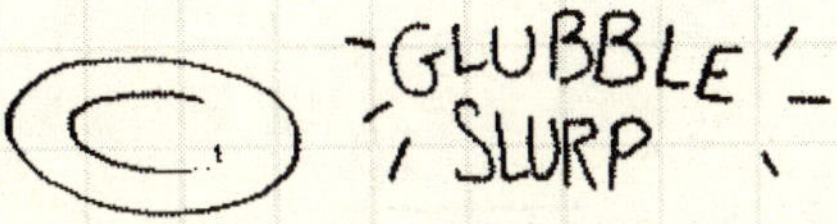

There were four separate sums to get to the answer, but you can save time by writing them all out together like this:

$$
\begin{array}{rr}
 & 12834 \\
\times & 217 \\
\hline
 & 2566800 \\
 & 128340 \\
 & 89838 \\
\hline
= & 2784978 \\
\hline
\end{array}
$$

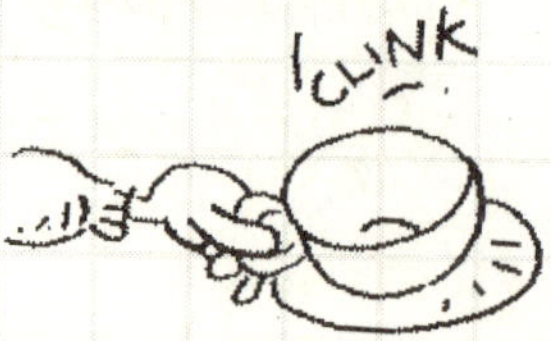

When you do each bit of multiplying, you write the answers down under each other, then add them up at the end.

So let's see if we've helped...

## The Grid Method

You can split big multiplying sums into lots of little sums by drawing a grid of boxes. Here's how we'd work out 439×27:

We split 439 into 400+30+9 and write it along the top. 27 becomes 20+7 and we write that down the side.

We then multiply each number along the top by each number down the side and write the answers in the boxes.

| | 400 | 30 | 9 |
|---|---|---|---|
| 20 | 8000 | 600 | 180 |
| 7 | 2800 | 210 | 63 |

If you're not sure where the answers in the middle came from, look at 2800. There's a 7 at the side and 400 on the top, so $7 \times 400 = 2800$.

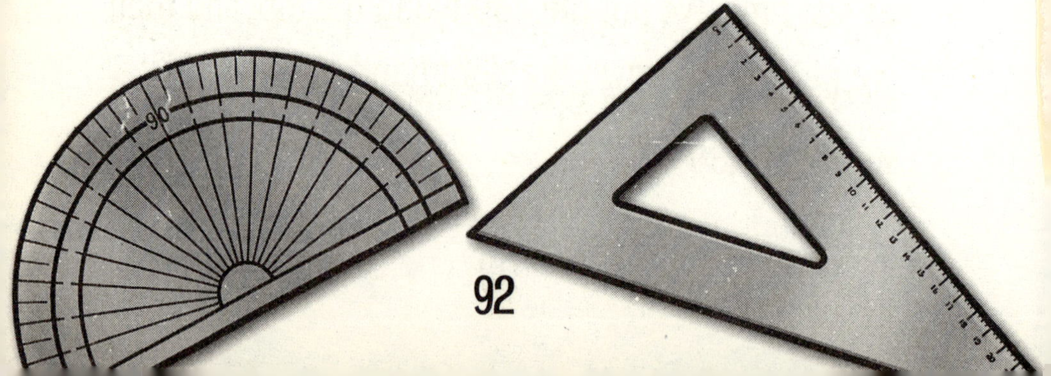

All we do now is add up all the numbers in the middle and get the answer!

```
 8000
  600
  180
 2800
  210
   63
-----
11853
```

## The Lattice Method

This one is really sneaky! You need to draw boxes with diagonal lines going through them. We'll work out 439×27 again to see if we get the same answer as last time. We put the 439 along the top, and then we put the 27 down the right hand side like this:

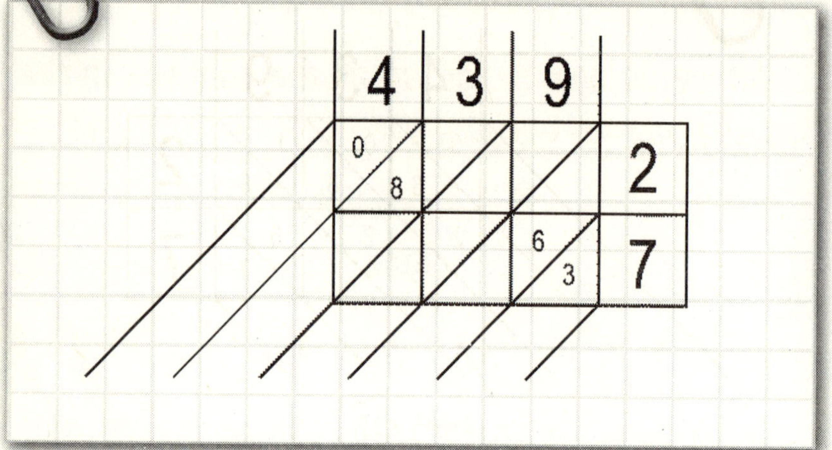


It's so exciting we've already started filling some of the middle in!

What we do is multiply the top digits by the side digits. Here you can see 9×7 = 63. We put the 63 in with one digit either side of the diagonal line. You'll also see that 4×2 = 8, so we write that as 08. When we've filled all the boxes we go down the diagonals and add all the numbers up.

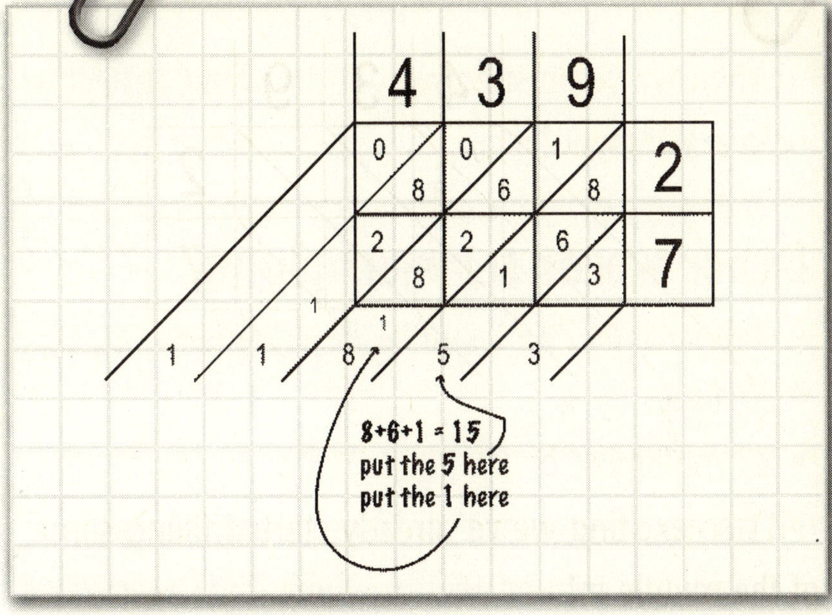


You have to concentrate when you do the adding!

The 3 was just on its own, so we didn't add it to anything. The next diagonal had 8+6+1 = 15. You'll see how we write the 5 in the answer, then put a little 1 in the next column. When we added that we got 1+6+2+8 … plus the extra 1 = 18. We write the 8 in the answer, and put the little 1 in the next column.

When we've finished we get the same answer as before. Whoopee!

## Other words for multiplying

A sum such as 27×9 can be described as

- 27 times by 9
- 27 multiplied by 9
- "twenty seven nines" or "nine twenty sevens"

If you are dealing with fractions then watch out for the word "of". Something like this $\frac{1}{5}\times40$ would usually be called "one fifth of forty". So "OF" also means "multiplied by".

## Is it all too easy?

We've already ZAPPED some pretty big sums, so are you feeling happy? Or are you getting suspicious? Is it all too easy? Is there something nasty waiting for us? Are you getting that kind of creepy feeling that comes when:

• you pick some socks off a shelf in the shop and realise they are just a little bit too warm and clammy

• you bite into an apple and see half a worm wiggling out of the other bit

• you sit down in the cinema and gradually realise that the seat is damp

• you're having a bath in an empty house and see the door handle start to turn

If you are getting a creepy feeling, then it's no wonder because we're about to look at dividing.

This is where even the most innocent little numbers suddenly become murderous! But we've come this far so there's no going back now. Get ready to hold your nose because we're going into...

# DASTARDLY DIVIDING

Once upon a time there was a nice ordinary number 6 playing with a jolly little 3.

First they played at adding…

6+3 = 9

…then they played at subtracting…

6–3 = 3

…then they had a go at multiplying…

6×3 = 18

…and finally the 6 made a suggestion.

"How about doing some dividing?" she asked.

"But I thought dividing was dangerous!" said the 3.

"Oh no!" said the 6. "Look for me on the tables and you will see that $3 \times 2 = 6$. If you divide into me, you will go two times like this…"

$6 \div 3 = 2$

"Brilliant!" said the 3. Dividing looked like fun after all!

Then along came a number 7.

“Can I play too?” said the 7.

“Of course,” said the others, and they all did some lovely sums together.

$6+7 = 13$     $7-3 = 4$     $7\times6 = 42$

$3\times7 = 21$     $3+7 = 10$     $7-6 = 1$

“That’s enough kid’s stuff,” said the 7. “Now then, who’s ready for some dividing?”

“ME!” cried the little 3. “I’ll divide into you, but how many times do I go?”

They looked at the tables.

“I only appear next to the 1 or another 7,” said the 7. “Maybe I can’t divide by 3.”

“That’s silly!” said the 3. “Let’s have a go anyway.”

So the 3 tried to divide into the 7.

$7\div3 = 2$ and 1 left over.

“Oh no!” said the 3. “I can go twice, but then

there is one more left over, and I can't divide into that!"

"Let me try," said the 6.

$7 \div 6 = 1$ and 1 left over.

"Gosh!" said the 6. "I get one left over too!"

"Pathetic!" sneered the 7. "You're not doing it properly! Let me divide into you, I'll show you!"

$6 \div 7 =$ but it wouldn't go!

"See?" said the 6. "It's not that easy is it?"

"You just wait," said the 7. "I'll try really hard this time."

And so the 7 tried as hard as he could.

He calculated, he carried over, he cancelled and suddenly there was an almighty explosion of decimals right across the field…

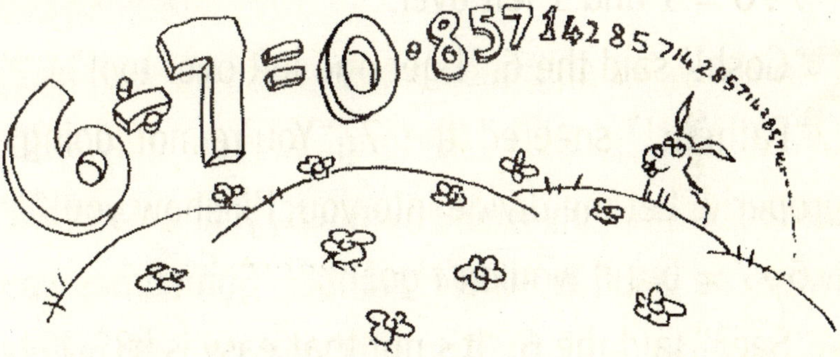


"Arghhh!" screamed the 6.

The 3 looked on in horror as she realized the awful truth. Sometimes dividing was fun, but other times it was murderous!

# WHAT'S WRONG WITH DIVIDING?

So far we've only seen whole numbers such as 2, 17 and 56,893. As long as you only add, subtract or multiply whole numbers, your answer will always be another whole number. Sometimes you can be lucky and dividing will end up with whole numbers, but usually you end up getting fractions.

Suppose you have been growing four clumps of hair on a big lump of old cheese and you decide it's time to share them out between three bald people.

Sharing is the same as dividing, so what we have is four clumps divided by three people which looks like this: 4÷3

To start with, everybody can have one clump each…

…but there will be one clump left over. You'll have to divide the last clump into three equal clumpettes. This is the same as one divided by three, or written in numbers it's 1÷3. But how big is one hairy clumpette?

Here's where the dividing sign is interesting, because there's a neat little trick that shows what it's trying to tell you: With dividing signs you can move the numbers onto the dots like this…

$$1 \div 3 \qquad 1 \div 3 \qquad \frac{1}{3}$$

If you write one over three, you get a fraction called a "third" so if the last clump is shared between our three people, they will each get one third of it. Each person already had one whole clump to start with, so they each end up with $1\frac{1}{3}$ clumps of hair, and suddenly they all look terribly gorgeous because people with hair always do.

Warning! Fractions can be a bit rude and naughty.

See? So just in case you are easily offended, we're going to lock them away until the next chapter.

## When you can't have fractions

Sometimes when you divide you don't get nice whole numbers *and* you are not allowed to have a fraction either. You just end up with little spare numbers left over that you haven't a clue what to do with.

Suppose you have seven nice cuddly hamsters and you want to share them between four people. To start with each person can have one nice cuddly hamster each...

...but what do we do with the three nice cuddly hamsters left in the box? You can either do this:

Or maybe Professor Fiendish could help:

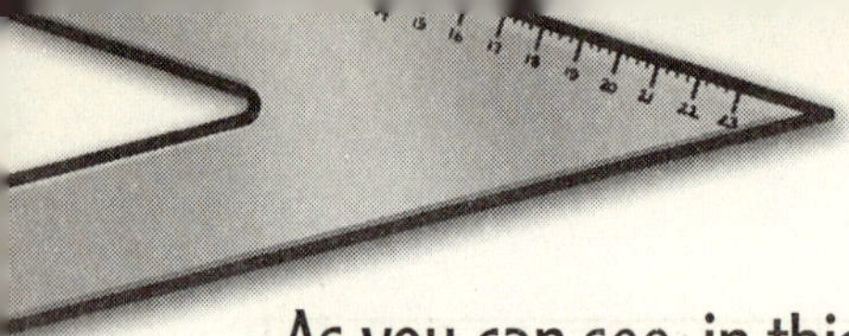

As you can see, in this case there are a few hamsters left over that we can't do anything with, and anything left over tends to be called the "remainder".

By now you will have realised that dividing is a nasty mean business, and so speaking of nasty mean things, it's time to introduce our very special guest star … Mr Titus O'Skinty!

Phew! Thank goodness he's given us an easy one to start with. Luckily for us we can find 21 on the times tables because 7×3 = 21. That means 21÷3 = 7.

Rats! If we're going to win anything we'll have to work a bit harder. A quick look at the tables tells us that 72 is the same as 8×9. This makes it easy if we wanted to divide by 8 or by 9, but that's no good because we want to divide by 4.

Yes, a lot of dividing sums do have short cuts, but if you can't see one then you have to work it out the long way. You need to write the sum out like this.

$4\overline{)72}$ ← the answer will come out on top

There are two weird things about dividing.

• When you divide, the answer comes out on the top, so make sure you leave a gap for it.

• With normal sums you always start working out the units, but when you're dividing you start at the other end!

We start by dividing the four into the seven. That's easy! $7 \div 4 = 1$ with remainder 3. (It's the same sum as when we divided 7 hamsters by 4 kids). We write the 1 above the seven and we write the remainder 3 in front of the 2 so we don't forget it.

$$\begin{array}{r} 1\phantom{^{3}2} \\ 4\overline{)7^{3}2} \end{array}$$

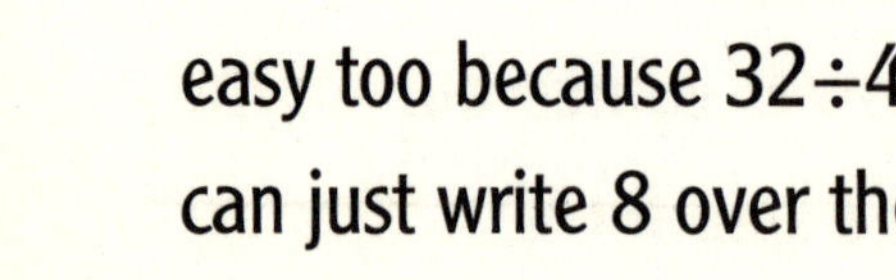


Now we move along and divide 4 into 32. That's easy too because $32 \div 4 = 8$ with no remainder. We can just write 8 over the 2 and we've finished!

$$\begin{array}{r} 18 \\ 4\overline{)7^{3}2} \end{array}$$

The answer is 18. YAY!

OK, Gladys, tell us your way of doing it!

## Chunking

Here's one more way of doing this sum! We start with 72 and see how many 4s we can take away until there's nothing left. We start like this:

72–4 = 68 then 68–4 = 64 then 64–4 = 60 … and so on. Of course this takes ages, but we can hurry it up.

We know that 4×10 = 40, so lets take away ten fours all at once. 72−40 = 32. Now we have 32 left which is the same as eight more 4's. So how many fours do we need to take away in total? It's 10+8 = 18. Done!

It doesn't matter which way we do the sum, we can tell Titus that the answer is 18.

## Long Division

629÷17 is a mean sum! There's no 17 on the tables and certainly there is no 629. Mind you, it would be nice to win £100, wouldn't it? So we're going to use something called LONG DIVISION. Wooo!

Unfortunately the crow is right. Never mind, we'll just start the same way as we did our 72÷4 sum earlier, and see how we get on.

First we write the sum out with a space on top for the answer.

$$17\overline{)6\,2\,9}$$

The fun thing about long division is that it involves a lot of guessing, so here's a handy tip: *use a pencil!*

Another fun thing is that 629 is too big to deal with all at once, so we'll cover the end up!

We now start with a simple little sum – how many times does 17 go into 6? Of course it won't go any times because 6 is a lot smaller than 17, and so you can write a 0 over the 6 if you like.

```
   0
17)629
```

Most people wouldn't bother putting the 0 in, but it isn't such a silly idea because it helps you write the next number in the correct place.

Now move along one place so we can see the tens column as well. Divide 17 into 62. It's time for our first guess! (You'll see how to make your guesses better in the *Rough Sums* chapter.)

```
   04
17)629
```

Let's guess that 17 goes into 62 four times. We write a 4 in the tens column. The tricky bit is working out the remainder! We need to multiply 4 by 17. It comes to 68 so we put that in underneath.

```
   04
17)629
   68
```

We then take 68 from 62 to see what the remainder is ... HANG ON! 68 is too big to take away from 62. You might want to shout out a naughty word.

Ha ha! Serves him right. Anyway, we now know that our guess of 4 was too big, so we'll rub out the 4 and the 68 and try dividing by 3 instead.

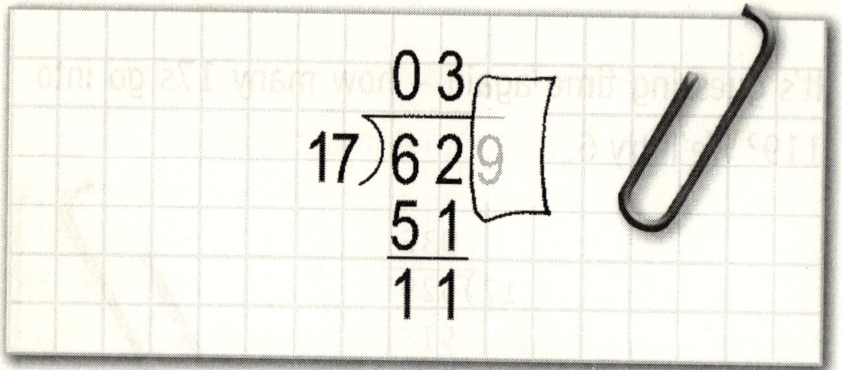


Now we multiply the 3 by the 17 and get 51. Take the 51 away from the 62 and we get 11. Next we move along to include the 9 from the units column. All you do is "drop it down" to join the other numbers on the bottom line.

It's guessing time again – how many 17s go into 119? We'll try 6.

```
      036
17 ) 629
      51
      ---
      119
      102
      ---
       17
```

We then multiply 6 by 17 to get 102, take that away from 119 and get a remainder of...17! That means that we could have divided one more 17 into 119.

Shout another naughty word. Go on, you know you want to.

Rub out the 6 in the answer and write 7, change the sums and you should get this:

```
     037
17)629
   51
   119
   119
    00
```

That's it! There's no remainder – we can say the answer is 37!

What do you think? Shall we play for the car? Why not? Let's face it, we're getting pretty good at this dividing lark.

It looks like Gladys has seen another short cut, but as we don't know about factors yet, we'll just steam in and smash this sum to bits. It won't take

long with our devastating combination of top tricks, bulging brains and heavenly good looks.

The sums come out like this:

```
      48
  91)4375
   - 364
   =  735
   -  728
        7
```

There are two things to notice here. The first is that 91 would not go into 4, then it would not go into 43, so our first guess was "how many times will 91 go into 437?". If you do a rough sum you get 400÷100 and you get the answer 4.

The second thing to notice is that we have a little 7 left over at the bottom! This is because 91 will not go into 4375 exactly, instead it goes 48 times with a remainder of 7.

We can't let him beat us now! Remember when we divided the last hairy clump into three pieces? We got $\frac{1}{3}$. Here we are dividing the last 7 into 91 pieces – so maybe we can just write it like this: $\frac{7}{91}$.

Thank goodness Gladys knows how to deal with fractions! You'll know what to do too when you read the next chapter, but first let's collect our prize...

BAH! TAKE THE CAR AWAY AND DONT COME BACK.
HUH! HE WON'T EVEN LEND YOU HIS SCISSORS!
CUT HERE
STAR PRIZE!

What a swizz! But at least we got something and what's more, we've nearly found out how a calculator makes decimal fractions. That surprised you, didn't it? You'll see more about that in the next chapter.

## Other ways that division slithers into your life

Division is probably the sneakiest thing in maths for suddenly turning up unexpectedly. If the sum you have to work out is 56÷8, sometimes it turns up obviously like this:

- 56 divided by 8
- 8s into 56

....but usually it's disguised by little innocent phrases such as:

- 56 over 8
- how many times can you take 8 from 56?

- how many 8s are there in 56?
- how many 8s can you get out of 56?
- what is 56 shared by 8?

Don't be fooled – they are all the same sum!

## The secret joke

You've now got through the toughest chapter in this book, so you deserve a bit of a treat. Remember back in the Secret Code chapter we mentioned a RUDE JOKE? Here it is:

What's invisible and smells of carrots?

The answer is ... 25 19 3 4 11 29 26 7 19 38 39

To decode the answer you need the KEY NUMBER which you have to work out by doing

this sum: 37557÷39. Don't use a calculator because that won't help! We don't want any lazy old clot who can prod a few buttons to know this great joke, it's only for people who can crack long divisions using their brains.

Start by writing it out like this:

$$39\overline{)37557}$$

Do the whole sum with all the working out until you finish up with 0 at the bottom. You then count up how many times the digits 1 and 2 appear in your calculations and that is the key number.

Good luck!

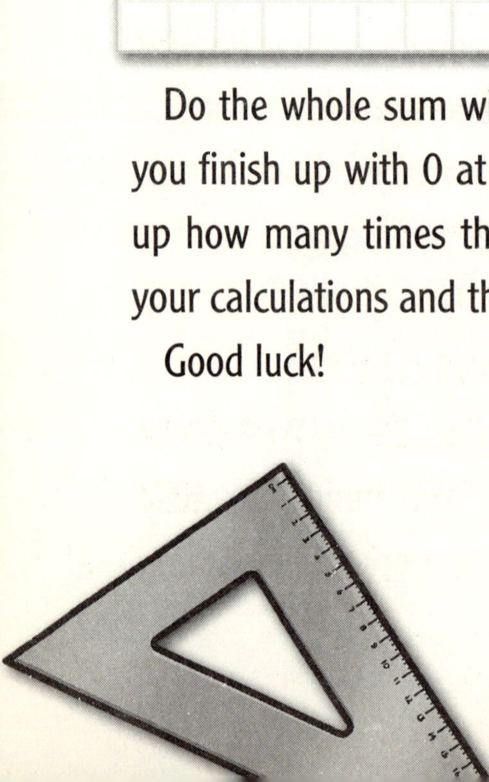

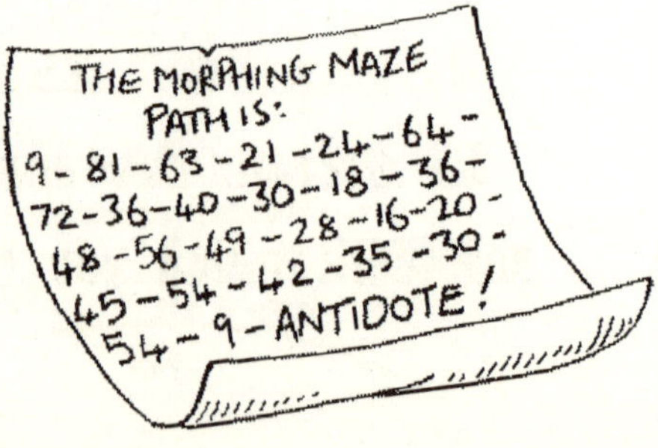

# NAUGHTY NUMBERS

Some numbers divide up nicely, but others are a bit naughty.

12 is a really nice number because you can divide it by 1, 2, 3, 4 and 6 without getting any remainder or a nasty fraction. This is why you can often buy things in twelves, because there are lots of neat ways of packing them in boxes.

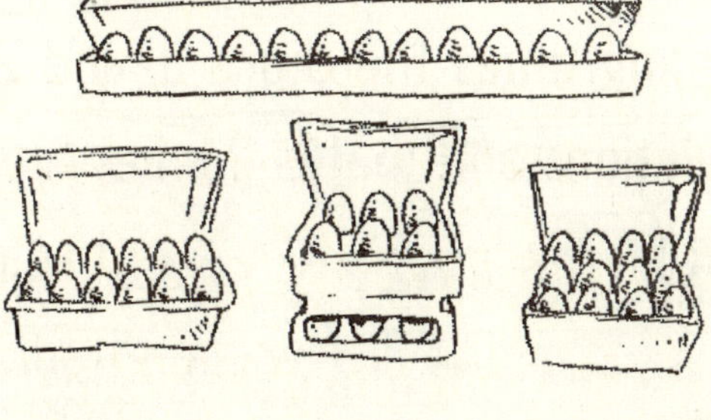

13 is a naughty number. Even though it's only one more than 12, it refuses to let you divide it up

neatly. There are only two numbers it will divide by without giving you a remainder or a fraction:

$13 \div 1 = 13$

$13 \div 13 = 1$

This means there's only one way of neatly packing 13 things into a box:

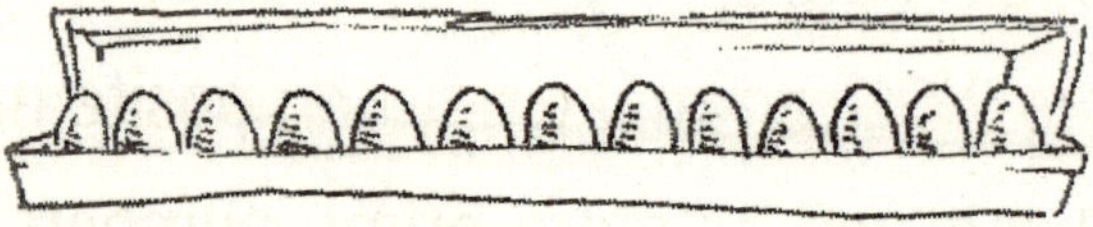

If you try boxes that are shorter and wider, you'll always end up with empty spaces, or things left over.

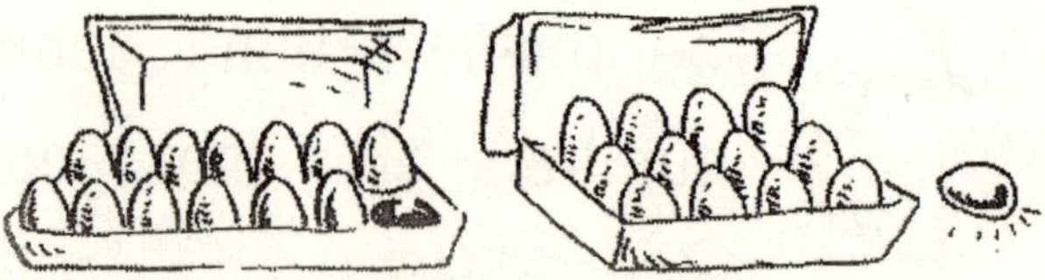

These naughty numbers that only divide by themselves and 1 are called PRIME NUMBERS and there are tons of them. The smallest prime number is 2, and next prime numbers are 3, 5, 7, 11, 13, 17, 19, 23, 29.... and the list goes on forever.

- 2 is the only even prime number
- You never find a prime number in the middle of the times tables – only round the edges
- Numbers that aren't prime are called composite numbers. You can make any composite number by multiplying two or more prime numbers together. For instance 84 = 2×2×3×7. Here we say that 2,2,3 and 7 are the prime factors of 84.

The funniest thing about prime numbers is that our pure mathematicians can't decide if 1 is prime or not...

I SAY, KIMPTON, I'VE JUST DECIDED THAT THE NUMBER 1 IS PRIME.
HOHO, WINCH, YOU ARE A CARD! OF COURSE 1 ISN'T PRIME.
BUT KIMPTON, THE CONCEPT OF 1 BEING PRIME IS SO BEAUTIFUL.
WHAT UTTER ROT! IF 1 WAS PRIME THEN THE WHOLE STRUCTURE OF NUMBERS COLLAPSES.
PRIME!
NOT PRIME!

We decided the fairest way to settle this argument was to do a survey of 100 million *Murderous Maths* readers. Here are the results:

## Is 1 a prime number?

| VOTES | |
|---|---|
| Yes | 7 |
| No | 8 |
| Don't know | 211 |
| Don't care | 99,999,774 |

The *Murderous Maths Organization* can now proudly declare that the number 1 is NOT prime by 8 votes to 7.

So that's that.

## How to make dividing sums shrink!

Here's a nasty little sum: 270÷18

Luckily we can make it a lot easier if we break each number down into its prime factors.

Let's do 18 first. We know that 18 = 6×3. We also know that 6 = 2×3, so if we put these all together we get 18 = 2×3×3.

Now we'll attack 270. Here's how you might work it out on paper!

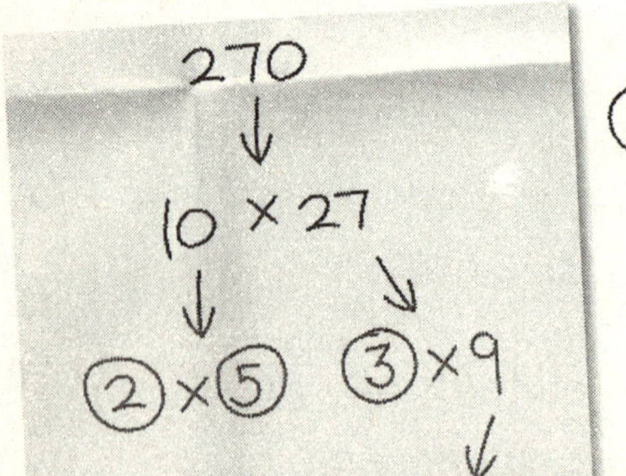

You'll see we did the obvious sum first and divided 270 into 10×27. We then kept dividing these numbers up until we got right down to the prime factors, and then we drew nice little rings round them. If we collect the factors up (the order doesn't matter) we know that 270 = 2×3×3×3×5.

Here comes the magic bit! We get our dividing sum 270÷18 and put one number over the other to it into a big ugly fraction.

$$\frac{270}{18} = \frac{2\times3\times3\times3\times5}{2\times3\times3}$$

Now we can cancel. This means if any number on the top has a matching number on the bottom, we can cross them both out!

$$\frac{\cancel{2}\times\cancel{3}\times\cancel{3}\times 3\times 5}{\cancel{2}\times\cancel{3}\times\cancel{3}} = 3\times 5 = 15$$

We're just left with 3×5 on the top, and that gives the answer 15, and that's it: 270÷18 = 15.

Remember Gladys talked about factorizing and reducing on page 125? This is what she'd spotted:

$$\frac{4375}{91} = \frac{7\times 625}{7\times 13} = \frac{\cancel{7}\times 625}{\cancel{7}\times 13} = \frac{625}{13}$$

Although she didn't worry about all the prime factors, she realized both numbers in the sum divided by 7. She could take the 7s out and *reduce* the sum. 625÷13 would give the same answer as 4375÷91, but it would be a lot easier to work out!

# FREAKY FRACTIONS

Fractions are the little bits you end up with when numbers don't divide neatly. You might think you can avoid them if you stick to sums with big numbers, but sadly that's not always true!

**Scene:** The abandoned gas station
**Place:** Red Ant Prairie, Illinois
**Date:** 24 July 1926 **Time:** 6.20 a.m.

The seven shady men gathered round the table and stared at the two old money bags lying next to the spluttering candle.

"There it is boys," said Blade. "Ten thousand dollars to split between the seven of us!"

"Why did you want us to meet up at the old gas station?" asked Weasel.

"We don't want people asking questions about where the money came from," said Blade.

"But we were just decorating Dolly Snowlip's house!" said Chainsaw Charlie.

There was an embarrassed silence.

"Nobody needs to know that!" hissed Blade. "We're supposed to be tough guys. If anyone asks, we held up a bank, right?"

"Right!" they all nodded.

"I wish we HAD held up a bank," groaned Half-Smile. "All that pink paint made me sick. I never want to see pink again as long as I live!"

"Never mind that," said Weasel. "Let's just make sure this dosh is split up absolutely fairly."

"Suits me," said Blade. "Or we'll just end up shooting holes in each other."

"What fraction do we each get?" asked Charlie.

"We don't need fractions!" laughed Blade. "Fractions are just for little numbers."

"Blade's right," said One-Finger Jimmy. "Let's just take a thousand each and see what's left."

All seven men took $1,000 each which was $7,000. That left $3,000 on the table.

"How do we split three thousand between seven?" asked big Porky. "Do we need fractions yet?"

"No way!" said Blade. "We split it into hundreds and share them out, and luckily we've got the right guy to work it out. How many do we get, Numbers?"

The smallest of the men had a quick think. "Three

thousand is thirty hundreds. We can take four hundred each, and that leaves two hundred on the table."

"At least it's in tens, singles and coins," said Porky. "How many tens do we get each, Numbers?"

"Two," said Numbers.

"Only two?" gasped Blade. "We only get two tens each out of two hundred dollars?"

"Is this some kind of dirty trick?" shouted One-Finger Jimmy, but then he found himself looking down the barrels of Half-Smile's triple-shot slug shooter.

"If my friend Numbers says it's two tens each, then it's two tens each," said Half-Smile.

"That's right!" said Numbers. "If all seven of us take \$20, that makes \$140. Out of the \$200 that leaves \$60. We can each take eight of that."

By this time each man had \$1,428, so in total they had $\$1,428 \times 7 = \$9,996$

"There's still four dollars left on the table," said Porky. "So what do we do now?"

"We split the four dollars into cents, I guess," said the Weasel.

"Oh lordy!" said Blade. "You mean even though we started with ten thousand dollars, we still have to mess about with a few little cents?"

"Four hundred cents to be accurate," said Numbers. "And we each get 57 of them."

After lots of shuffling coins around and counting, each man checked his pile.

"I got $1,428 and 57 cents exactly," said Half-Smile.

"Me too," said Jimmy. "It's the same for all of us, but what do we do about THAT?"

Jimmy was pointing his one finger at the middle of the table. A final little one cent coin glinted in the candlelight.

"I guess I get my chainsaw and chop it into seven tiny pieces," said Charlie.

"No way!" snapped Blade. "I'm not messing with little bitty fractions of a cent. To save arguments, I'll take it."

He picked up the coin, only to find Half-Smile's slug shooter pointing at him.

"Put that back!" demanded Half-Smile.

"Never!" said Blade and he ran out of the door.

"Get after him!" shouted Weasel to Chainsaw.

"Get after them!" shouted Jimmy to Porky.

"After you!" shouted Porky, because he was polite.

They all charged out into the night, but on the way one of them kicked the table and knocked the candle over. It was a simple chain of events: upset candle, burning banknotes, oil-soaked timber, forgotten fuel bunker…

The seven men span round to see a giant orange fireball light up the sky.

"The gas station!" they cried. "And our MONEY!"

And that just goes to show, even when you're dividing up great big numbers, you still can't ignore those freaky little fractions.

There are two sorts of fractions – vulgar and decimal. We're going to look at vulgar fractions first, but be warned! As you know, the people in the *Murderous Maths* factory don't mind having a rude joke or two, but just occasionally things get out of control. If you are a nice person who is easily shocked, we suggest you close your eyes and block your ears before you read on.

## Vulgar Fractions

Vulgar fractions have a number on the top (called a numerator) and a number on the bottom (called a denominator). These fractions tend to be a bit cheeky, as you'll see when we invite a few onto the page...

Most fractions have the smaller number on the top and they describe "a bit of something". If you've got a bar of chocolate, and your evil brother tells you he's eaten a fraction of it, here's a rough guide to how greedy he's been:

- If the top number is a lot smaller than the bottom number, then the fraction is describing a very little bit. (So if he ate $\frac{1}{16}$ then that wasn't much.)
- If the top is nearly as big as the bottom, then the fraction is describing a big bit. (If he ate $\frac{11}{13}$ then that was most of it!)
- If the top is the same as the bottom, then the fraction equals 1. If your brother tells you he's eaten twenty-three twenty-thirds of the chocolate (i.e. $\frac{23}{23}$ ) then shove some spiders in his bed because he's eaten ALL OF IT!

There was also a strange fraction on the last page. Did you spot it? Here it is again...

If the number on the top is bigger than the bottom, then it's an improper vulgar fraction! So what's this one worth? Is it bigger than 5? Smaller than 20?

How rude! That's why it's usually best to get rid of them, so let's teach this one a lesson. Quick, grab it!

All we do is divide the bottom into the top so we get 58÷9 which gives us 6 with a remainder of 4. This means our improper $\frac{58}{9}$ becomes 6 with $\frac{4}{9}$ths left over. Let's have a look at it now.

There's still a little vulgar fraction left, but now that we have a big "6" next to it, we have a better idea of what the whole thing is worth – in this case, it's "six and a bit". This mixture of a whole number and a vulgar fraction is called a mixed fraction.

You can also turn a mixed fraction such as $6\frac{4}{9}$ back to being improper. Multiply the whole number 6 by the 9 on the bottom, then add the answer to the 4 on the top. Here we get $6 \times 9 = 54$, then $54+4 = 58$. We just put the 58 over the 9 and there we are, all improper again.

## Names of fractions

This is easy. Look at the number underneath, and that's how you get the name. $\frac{1}{5}$ is one fifth, $\frac{1}{12}$ is one twelfth, $\frac{1}{284}$ is one two hundred and eighty fourth and so on. There are just three exceptions:

$\frac{1}{2}$ is called a **half**. If you already knew that, you can have a big kiss for being so clever...

... but you don't have to if you don't want.

$\frac{1}{4}$ is called a **quarter**. This comes from the old Latin word "quartus" which means "fourth". In the old days bad people used to be hung, drawn and quartered, which meant they got chopped up. Mind you, there were usually more than four bits by the time the executioner had finished all his encores and curtain calls.

$\frac{1}{100}$ is called one **per cent**. This comes from Latin too, as *cent* means 100 and *per* means "divided by", so one per cent is one divided by 100. Percentages have a special sign which is % and there's more about them on page 171.

## Dividing cakes

Fractions can be used to describe bits of anything, but most people explain fractions by cutting cakes up into equal pieces like this:

And we're supposed to believe that's what happens in real life. Of course, what REALLY happens next is this:

Oh well, cakes are still the easiest way to see about fractions so we'll get a cake and see how we get on.

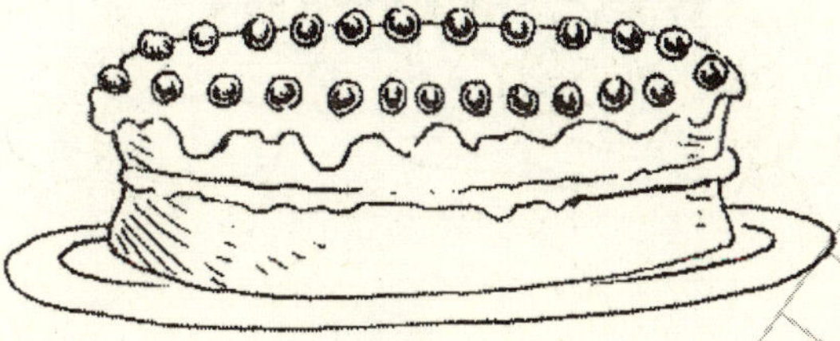

Our cake has 24 cherries round the top. We'll mark it into three equal pieces and cut one of them out. By now you've realised that this piece is one third of the whole cake, and so we should be able to work out how many cherries are on it. What makes it fun is that there are two ways of doing this.

- As we divided our cake by 3, the number of cherries we get on one piece is $24 \div 3$
- As we have one third of a cake, we can just multiply $24 \times \frac{1}{3}$. Remember that "of" means "multiply by."

Of course both answers come to eight cherries, which you can see when you look at the cake.

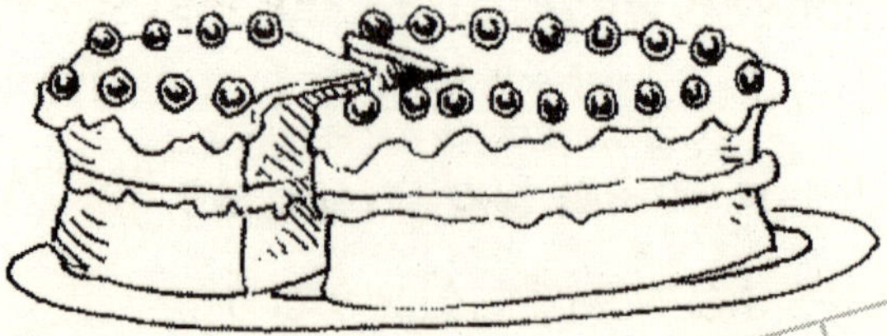

This shows you that $24 \div 3$ is the same as $24 \times \frac{1}{3}$. In other words dividing by 3 is the same as multiplying by $\frac{1}{3}$.

Here's another cake with 21 cherries on it, and we've divided it into seven bits:

If we eat two sevenths of the cake, how many cherries do we get?

Simple – each piece of cake is one seventh of the cake, so we'll be eating two of them. The sum is $21 \times \frac{2}{7}$. That's not too bad to work out. We can see that one seventh is $21 \div 7 = 3$ which tells us that each piece has three cherries. If we eat two pieces, we get $2 \times 3 = 6$ cherries. That's the answer: $21 \times \frac{2}{7} = 6$.

## Making fractions simpler

Suppose you have a box of 12 eggs.

You throw away six of them.

What fraction of your eggs have you got left? There are two ways of looking at this:

- As you started with twelve eggs and now have six, the fraction is six twelfths, or $\frac{6}{12}$.
- You can also see that you have half of the box left or $\frac{1}{2}$.

So which fraction is right $\frac{6}{12}$ or $\frac{1}{2}$?

In fact they are both the same thing!

You don't have to throw eggs away to work this out. If you have a fraction like $\frac{6}{12}$, see if you can find a number that divides into the top and the bottom. In this case 6 will divide into both so that's what you do.

$$\frac{6}{12} = \frac{6 \div 6}{12 \div 6} = \frac{1}{2}$$

Let's start with the full box again, but this time you throw away four eggs.

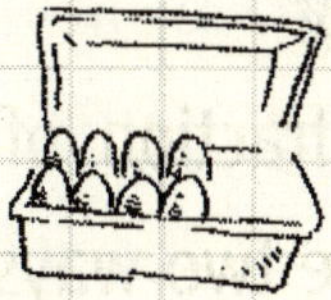

What fraction have you got left?

In this case it's $\frac{8}{12}$, but we can make this neater too. Both 8 and 12 will divide by 4 so that's what we do.

$$\frac{8}{12} = \frac{8 \div 4}{12 \div 4} = \frac{2}{3}$$

We have two thirds of our eggs left!

When you make fractions simpler like this it's called reducing. It's just like what we did back on page 140.

## Decimals

If you catch your calculator doing something naughty (for instance it might be chatting up the TV remote control) you can punish it by making it turn some vulgar fractions into *decimals.* Let's try an easy fraction first: $\frac{1}{10}$.

We know that $\frac{1}{10}$ means $1 \div 10$, and if you put that into your calculator you get 0·1. The important bit is the little dot.

To explain this we need Wally the 1.

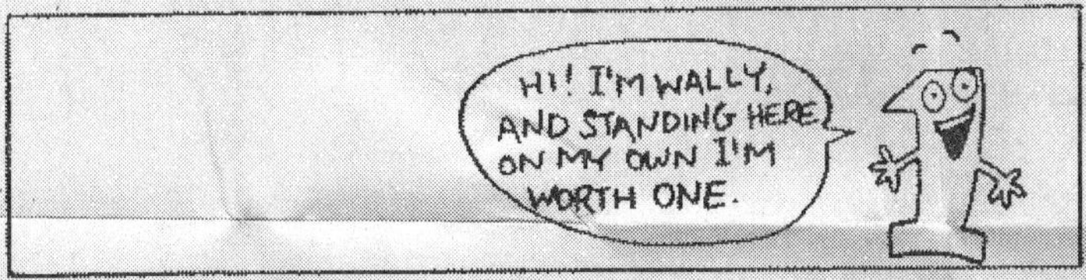


Here's what happens if we move him along to the left one place and write a zero.

Here's what happens if we write in a second zero:

We can move him along as far as we like...

But now we need to get him back to where he started so he's just worth 1 again, then we'll try to move him the other way!

That's the decimal point. As soon as Wally moves over it, he turns into a fraction. Every place he moves he's worth ten times less.

Wally is right, because he is now standing in the "tenths" place. By the way, you'll notice that we have put a "0" in front of the decimal point. We could have just left it as ·1 but because decimal points are so teeny, we put a 0 in front so that we don't forget it's there.

Thank you Wally, that was lovely. Now we'll bring in some other numbers. If you have a number like 25·378, this is what it's worth:

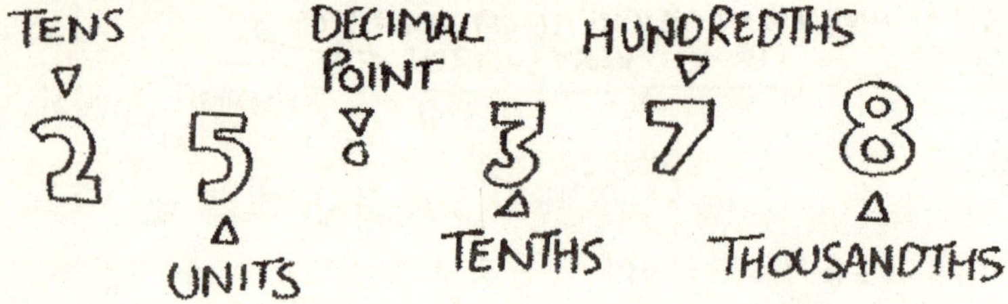


By now you will have realised how important the decimal point is. If you send an order for 25·378 ice creams, it means you want twenty-five whole ice creams and little bit more.

But what happens if you forget to put the decimal point in?

## When calculators get dangerous

Now let's see what the calculator does with a harder decimal fraction.

Suppose we were going to work out 19÷8, we would find 8 goes into 19 two times, and we'd have a remainder of three. As humans are jolly sensible, we could write the answer like this $2\frac{3}{8}$, and decide we've done enough. Calculators are not as clever as us for two reasons:

- calculators don't usually write vulgar fractions
- calculators never know when to stop

Here's how the sum for 19÷8 would look if a calculator did it on paper:

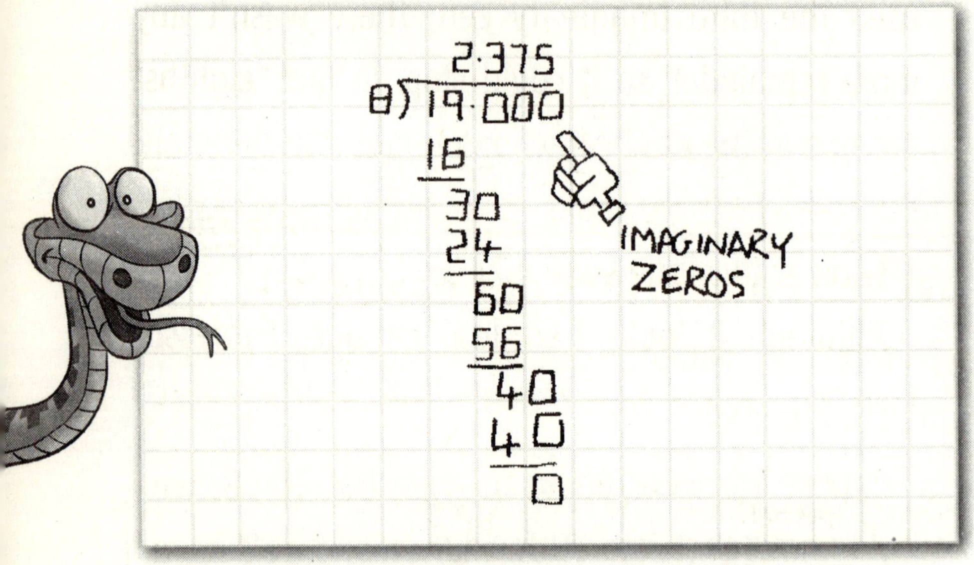


Instead of a remainder of 3, the calculator keeps on dividing. To do that it needs to imagine there are some extra zeros and bring them down to help with the sum! At least it does do one sensible thing – as soon as it starts imagining zeros, it puts a decimal point in the answer. Here the calculator has converted the $2\frac{3}{8}$ into a decimal which is 2·375.

The calculator was lucky here because after it had used the third imaginary zero there wasn't any more remainder, so it could stop. In fact "eighths" are one of the easier fractions to put into decimals, but some fractions make your calculator go mad.

Look at this little sum: 17÷3.

Although it looks harmless enough, Professor Fiendish can use it for one of his diabolical plans!

SOON NOBODY WILL BE ABLE TO MOVE BECAUSE OF MY INFINITE PROGRESSION OF SIXES!
CHUG CHUG CHUG
5.66666
NOT SO FAST, PROFESSOR! JUST A QUICK BIT OF CANCELLATION AND CONVERSION.
CHUG CHUG CHUG CHUG
MURDEROUS MATHS READER
YOUR SIXES ARE REDUCED TO A SIMPLE VULGAR FRACTION. NOW GO IN PEACE AND TROUBLE US NO MORE!
BAH!
PTHHT

Although the calculator kept bringing down more and more zeros, it could never get rid of the remainder. Even if the screen stretched all the way to the moon, the sixes would still go off the end. That's why sometimes it's better to have vulgar fractions even though they can be a bit naughty.

## Money

Money uses its own form of decimals. If you have £7·23, that means you have seven pounds and twenty three hundredths of a pound. As there are 100 pennies in a pound, twenty three hundredths is the same as 23p.

Suppose you have £3·78263726545. Obviously you've got three pounds, but how many pennies have you got? The answer is 78p, because money can only deal with two numbers after the decimal point. Sadly the other 0.00263726545 of a pound will be wasted and lost for ever.

## % = Per cent

Percent means "divide by 100", so if you have 50%, then that means $\frac{50}{100}$. If you wanted you could divide top and bottom by 50 and so make 50% into $\frac{1}{2}$ and it means the same thing. 100% is the same as $\frac{100}{100}$ and means "one" or "the whole thing". Percents are also very easy to write in decimals, you just put the number behind the decimal point. Therefore 50% is the same as 0·50, but you don't need to write the last zero so it's 0·5. Watch out for very small percents though – if the percent only has a single digit such as 3%, you have to put a zero in front like this: 3% = 0·03.

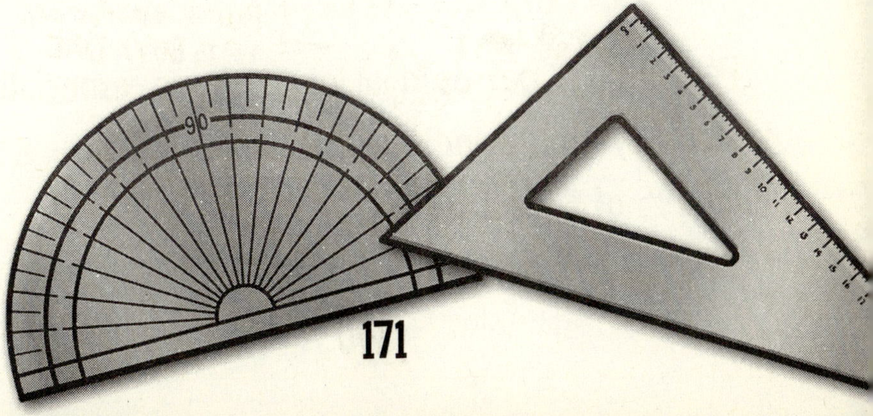

Here are some common fractions, decimals and percentages:

| Fraction | Decimal | Per Cent |
|---|---|---|
| 1 | 1·0 | 100% |
| $\frac{1}{2}$ | 0·5 | 50% |
| $\frac{1}{3}$ | 0·333 | 33% |
| $\frac{2}{3}$ | 0·667 | 67% |
| $\frac{1}{4}$ | 0·25 | 25% |
| $\frac{3}{4}$ | 0·75 | 75% |
| $\frac{1}{5}$ | 0·2 | 20% |
| $\frac{1}{8}$ | 0·125 | 12·5% |
| $\frac{1}{10}$ | 0·1 | 10% |
| $\frac{1}{100}$ | 0·01 | 1% |

Percentages get used a lot in shops, especially when they are having a sale. Because 100p = £1, then 1% of £1 is 1 penny.

Suppose you're buying some pants for £5, but it turns out they are not perfectly new, so the shop takes 30% off.

What will you save?

• 30% off means that for every £1 you would normally pay, you save 30p. As the pants were £5, you would save 5×30p which is £1.50.

• OR ... you can say 30% = 0·3, so the amount you save is £5×0·3 = £1·50.

What will the pants cost?

• If you save £1·50 then the pants cost £5-£1·50 = £3·50.

• OR ... the full cost of the pants is 100%, so if you save 30%, you still have to pay 100%-30% = 70%. As 70% = 0·7, then the pants will cost £5×0·7 = £3·50

## Sums with fractions

People get really confused by sums with fractions, unless you know all the sneaky secrets.

### Sneaky Secret 1 – Multiplying a whole number by a fraction

You just times the top of the fraction by the whole number, then put the answer over the bottom.

$$4 \times \frac{7}{12} = \frac{4 \times 7}{12} = \frac{28}{12}$$

You could leave it like that, but if you're feeling clever you'll see we can reduce it because 4 will divide into both numbers!

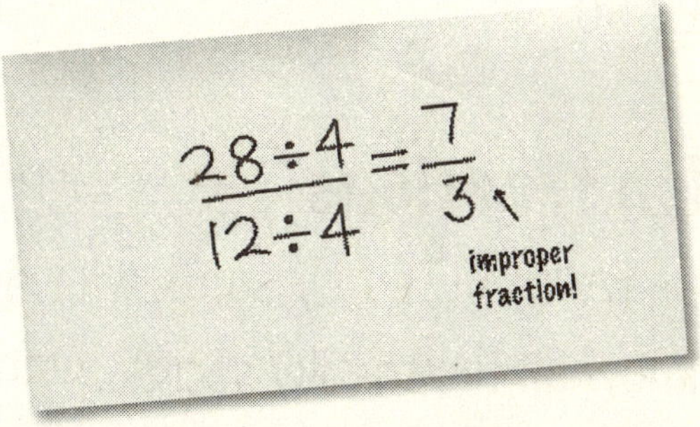


That looks neater, but just to be really clever, we'll make the improper fraction into a mixed fraction. Remember, we divide the 7 by 3, then put the remainder on the top…

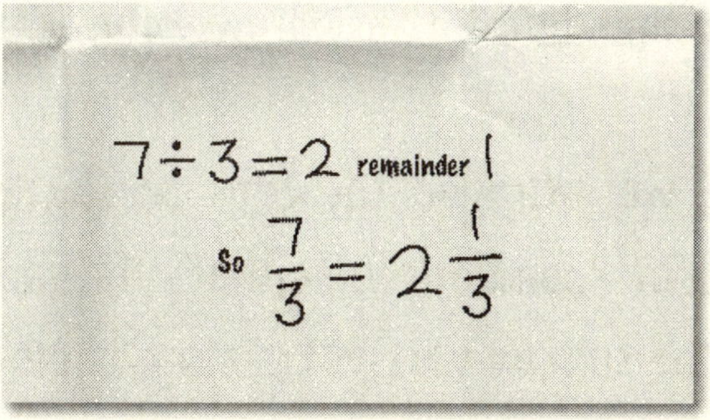

## Sneaky Secret 2 – Multiplying two fractions together

This is easy! You just multiply the tops and the bottoms.

$$\frac{3}{7} \times \frac{2}{11} = \frac{3 \times 2}{7 \times 11} = \frac{6}{77}$$

The fun part here is that when you multiply with fractions, you can swap the tops over. This can give you some sneaky short cuts! Look at this one:

$$\frac{2}{5} \times \frac{5}{9} = \frac{5}{5} \times \frac{2}{9} = 1 \times \frac{2}{9} = \frac{2}{9}$$

Here we swapped the tops so that we got a fraction of $\frac{5}{5}$, and of course that's the same as 1. It made the sum very easy! Let's see another:

$$\frac{4}{5} \times \frac{3}{8} = \frac{3}{5} \times \frac{4}{8} = \frac{3}{5} \times \frac{1}{2} = \frac{3}{10}$$

this reduces to this

Here we put the 4 over the 8, and the fraction then reduced to $\frac{1}{2}$, which made the final sum a LOT easier!

**Sneaky Secret 3 – Dividing by fractions**

This is SO easy, but hardly anybody remembers what to do! *You just turn the second fraction upside down and multiply!*

$$\frac{5}{8} \div \frac{2}{3} = \frac{5}{8} \times \frac{3}{2} = \frac{5 \times 3}{8 \times 2} = \frac{15}{16}$$

Turn upside down and multiply

Multiplying and dividing by fractions is quite easy, but adding fractions can be very strange as you're about to see!

## The phantom sausage

WAIT! Let's work it out with some maths first. What we are doing here is adding $\frac{1}{2} + \frac{1}{2}$. The BIG MISTAKE that a lot of people make is to add the tops togther and the bottoms together. If we do that, here's what we get:

$$\frac{1}{2} + \frac{1}{2} = \frac{1+1}{2+2} = \frac{2}{4} \times$$

WRONG!

You'll see we end up with $\frac{2}{4}$ which is two quarters. If we reduce this fraction by dividing the top and bottom by 2, see what we get!

$$\frac{2 \div 2}{4 \div 2} = \frac{1}{2}$$

So what has gone wrong?

Let's use a secret weapon here... *common sense!* If we add half a sausage to another half, we get two halves, and two halves make a whole sausage. Our sums should have looked like this:

$$\frac{1}{2} + \frac{1}{2} = \frac{1+1}{2} = \frac{2}{2} = 1 \quad \checkmark$$

**RIGHT!**

## Sneaky Secret 4 – Adding and taking away fractions

As we've just seen with the sausage, when you add fractions, *you just add the tops together, but keep the same bottom!*

But what do you do if the bottoms are different? You have to make their bottoms the same!

This will make more sense when we go and spy on the lovely Veronica Gumfloss in the pizza restaurant.

Even though Veronica is terribly lovely, she doesn't realise that if the pizza is cut into six, the pieces will be bigger than if it is cut into eight. Pongo McWhiffy has also ordered a pizza which is cut into eight pieces. He decides to dazzle Veronica with his manly charm.

Veronica agrees to swap, so who ends up eating more pizza?

- The lovely Veronica?
- Pongo?
- They both eat exactly the same?

Before we work out the exact answer, you might be able to spot a sneaky short cut. $\frac{1}{6}$ of a pizza is bigger than $\frac{1}{8}$ of a pizza, isn't it? So if Veronica is gives away $\frac{1}{6}$ of a pizza and gets $\frac{1}{8}$ of a pizza in return, she's going end up eating less!

Now let's do some sums to see exactly how much pizza each person eats.

Veronica's pizza was cut into six, but she only ate five of them which is $\frac{5}{6}$ of her own pizza. However, she did get a bit of Pongo's pizza in return, but Pongo's pizza was cut into eight, so he gave her $\frac{1}{8}$ of his. Although Veronica got to eat six bits of pizza altogether, did she have...

- $\frac{6}{6}$ of a pizza or
- $\frac{6}{8}$ of a pizza?

In fact these answers are both wrong! You can't add one eighth to five sixths because they've got *different bottoms*. Here's the sum to work out:

$\frac{5}{6}+\frac{1}{8}$

What we have to do is convert these fractions so they both have the same number on the bottom. The secret is to *multiply the top and bottom of each fraction by the other fraction's bottom!*

$$\frac{5}{6} \times \frac{8}{8} = \frac{40}{48} \qquad \frac{1}{8} \times \frac{6}{6} = \frac{6}{48}$$

Now we can see Veronica had $\frac{40}{48}$ of her own pizza and $\frac{6}{48}$ of Pongo's pizza. The good news is that now they have the same bottom so we can add them together!

$$\frac{40}{48} + \frac{6}{48} = \frac{46}{48}$$

There's just one last thing to do to make it neat – we can divide the top and bottom by 2.

$$\frac{46 \div 2}{48 \div 2} = \frac{23}{24}$$

This means that Veronica has eaten $\frac{23}{24}$ of a pizza, which is slightly less than a whole pizza.

We can now do the sum for Pongo. He eats seven of his eight pieces, plus one of Veronica's six pieces so he gets $\frac{7}{8}+\frac{1}{6}$ but we don't have to work this one out!

There's another EASY short cut. We know there were two whole pizzas to start with, and Veronica got $\frac{23}{24}$ of a pizza, so Pongo must have got what was left over.

Pongo got $2-\frac{23}{24}$ pizzas!

To work this sum out we can convert one of the whole pizzas into twenty fourths so instead of 2 pizzas we have $1\frac{24}{24}$. It's now easy to take away the amount of pizza that Veronica got and see what Pongo got:

$1\frac{24}{24}-\frac{23}{24} = 1\frac{1}{24}$

This tells us that Pongo got a complete pizza plus a little bit extra.

## How to compare fractions

It's always handy to know about fractions, even when you're whizzing across space. Suppose you run out of fuel and land on a rather smelly green moon. Some friendly mushrooms direct you to an old shed with a sign saying "Fiendish Fuels".

Oh no! How did HE get here?

Sure enough the professor comes out.

"Har har!" he says. "I've got lots of fuel cans, but you can only pick ONE. The cans are all the same size, and the fractions tell you how full they are. Only the fullest can will get you home again! If you pick the wrong can you'll drift off and be lost in deep space for EVER!"

So which can has got the biggest fraction on it?

To start off we'll compare two cans at a time, and eliminate the one which holds less. That way we'll quickly get rid of some of them.

Look at the two cans holding $\frac{9}{13}$ and $\frac{10}{13}$. Obviously the $\frac{10}{13}$ holds more, so we get rid of the $\frac{9}{13}$ can. These fractions were easy to compare because they were both "thirteenths" – in other words they both had 13 on the bottom. But how do we compare fractions with different bottoms?

There's a $\frac{16}{33}$ can and a $\frac{16}{21}$ can. $\frac{1}{33}$ is smaller than $\frac{1}{21}$, so if you have sixteen of each, the $\frac{16}{33}$ will be smaller so we can get rid of that one.

We can compare some of these cans using common sense. Let's try $\frac{2}{3}$ and $\frac{3}{4}$. If you think about it, the $\frac{2}{3}$ can has one third *missing*, and the $\frac{3}{4}$ can has one quarter *missing*. One quarter is smaller than one third, so the $\frac{3}{4}$ can has less missing – in other words it holds more! So we can get rid of the $\frac{2}{3}$ can.

So far then we've eliminated the $\frac{9}{13}$ , the $\frac{16}{33}$ and the $\frac{2}{3}$ cans.

Now we'll try a clever way to compare the $\frac{7}{9}$ can and the $\frac{10}{13}$ can. We're going to give them the same bottoms, just like when we added fractions back on page 184. Remember, we multiply the top and bottom of each fraction by the other fraction's bottom.

$$\frac{7}{9} \times \frac{13}{13} = \frac{91}{117} \qquad \frac{10}{13} \times \frac{9}{9} = \frac{90}{117}$$

The $\frac{7}{9}$ comes out as $\frac{91}{117}$ but the $\frac{10}{13}$ only comes out as $\frac{90}{117}$ . As the bottoms are the same, we can see $\frac{90}{117}$ is smaller, so we can get rid of the $\frac{10}{13}$ can.

The three cans left are $\frac{7}{9}$, $\frac{16}{21}$ and $\frac{3}{4}$ .

We could do some more sums like the last one, but now we'll use the quickest way to compare – even if it seems a bit like cheating! We turn these fractions into decimals using a calculator.

$\frac{7}{9} = 7 \div 9 = 0{\cdot}77777$

$\frac{16}{21} = 16 \div 21 = 0{\cdot}76190$

$\frac{3}{4} = 3 \div 4 = 0{\cdot}75$

We can see 0·77777 is the biggest so the $\frac{7}{9}$ can is the fullest!

Let's blast off and hope for the best!

Even though decimals can be a bit long and messy, they do make adding up different fractions easier. You just turn your fractions into decimals, then add them, but make sure the decimal points are all in the same column above and below each other! Here's a sum adding some decimal fractions:

$$\begin{array}{r} 0{\cdot}5294 \\ 0{\cdot}9130 \\ +\ 0{\cdot}375\phantom{0} \\ \hline =\ 1.8174 \\ \hline \end{array}$$

If you think that looks a bit nasty, here's something even nastier:

There, the decimals aren't so bad after all, are they?

# ROUNDING OFF

Here's a very strange man!

Nobody cares exactly how many flies he's got, so we'd usually "round the number off."

Suppose we round 31,862 to *four significant digits*. This means we just use the first four digits, then replace the last one with a zero. We get 31,860.

If we round it to *three significant digits* we could put 31,800. However it would be better to put

31,900, because this number line shows that 31,862 is closer to 31,900 than 31,800.

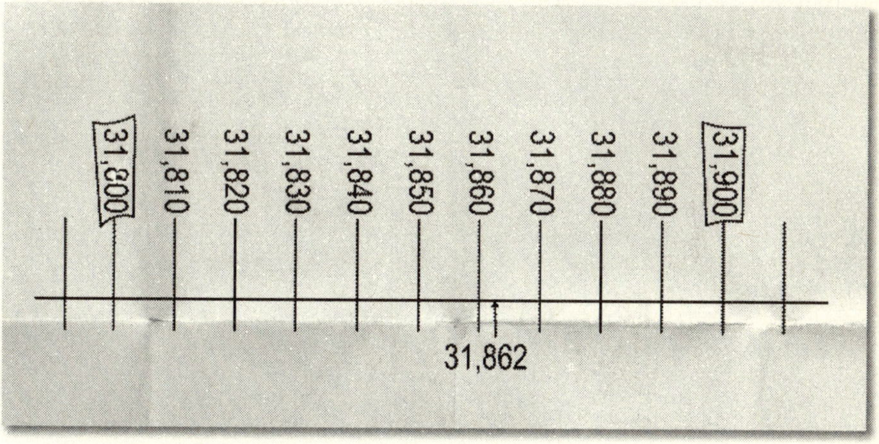


Here's the secret to rounding off:

If the next digit would have been 5 or higher, add 1 to the last digit.

The next digit after 318 would have been a 6, so we should add 1 to the 8 to make 9. Therefore:

31,862 rounded to three digits would be 31,900.

31,862 rounded to two digits would be 32,000.

And 31,862 rounded to just one digit would be 30,000. This number is much simpler to look at, but it still gives us a good idea of what the cow shed is like. YUK.

Is this lady telling us there are exactly 42,000 dung beetles in her pigsty? No, she's probably rounded it off to two digits! The exact answer could be any number between 41,500 and 42,499.

When you round numbers off, don't bother trying to be too accurate again. This rather good joke explains why:

ONE DAY AT THE MUSEUM.
HOW OLD IS THIS DINOSAUR?
SEVENTY MILLION YEARS AND TWO WEEKS
HOW DO YOU KNOW?
WHEN I STARTED HERE, THEY TOLD ME IT WAS SEVENTY MILLION YEARS OLD, AND I'VE BEEN WORKING HERE FOR TWO WEEKS

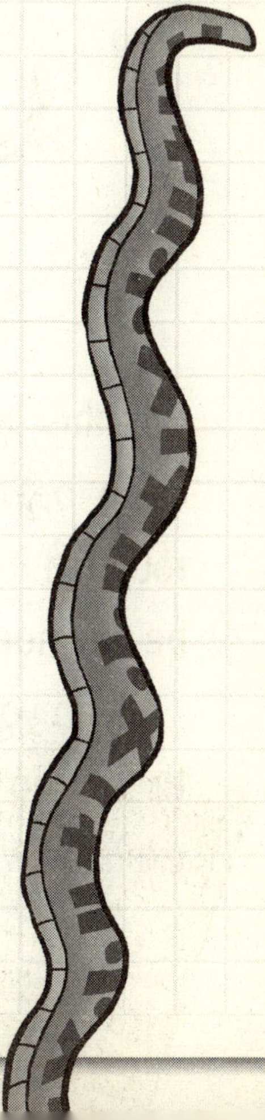

## How lazy are you?

If you work out $\frac{14}{17}$ as a decimal fraction on a big calculator you might get 0·82352941176470588235294117647 but how much should you write down?

**0·8**
Just one decimal place? It's amazing you can even be bothered to breathe.

**0·82**
Two decimal places means you probably don't bother getting undressed to get in the bath.

**0·823**
Three decimal places is better but it would have been even better if you'd written down…

**0·824** …because you used the rounding off rule! In this case the next digit would have been a 5 so you should have rounded the 3 up to a 4.

**0·82352941117657** Most people think that three digits is fine but some people simply can't get enough!

# ROUGH SUMS AND GOING MENTAL

Sometimes it's useful just to get an approximate answer to a sum, especially if you're in a hurry. Blade and his gang want to add up a lot of money very quickly, so let's help.

Here's the sum:

$$\begin{array}{r} 2346 \\ 3988 \\ 332 \\ +\ 5024 \end{array}$$

The best way to get a rough answer is to round the numbers off to two digits. You get 2300+4000+300+5000 = 11,600 which isn't too hard.

## Rough Subtracting

Here's the sum

```
  11690
-  2471
```

No problems! You can round the numbers off to get 11700-2500 which gives an answer of about 9200. If you want to round the numbers off even more roughly, there are a couple of tricks:

For adding or multiplying, round one number up and the other one down.

For subtracting or dividing, round both numbers up or round them both down.

In this case we are subtracting, so we'll round both numbers up and get 12000-3000 which gives us an answer of about 9000.

## Rough times

Here's the sum:

$$\begin{array}{r} 9219 \\ \times \quad 173 \end{array}$$

The secret of rough multiplying is to cross some of the end digits off (but keep count of how many have gone!) Let's make the sum into this:

$$\begin{array}{r} 92 \\ \times \quad 17 \end{array}$$

We've crossed off two numbers from the top line and one from the bottom, so that makes three crossed off numbers altogether. Write a big 3 on your nose or somewhere so you don't forget.

As we're multiplying, we'll round one number up and the other one down. We'll round the 92 up to

100 because that's a really nice rough number to work with. As we've rounded the 92 up, we ought to round the 17 down but be careful! If we round it right down to 10, we've almost chopped it in half! We'll just round it down to 16, so the sum becomes $16 \times 100 = 1{,}600$.

Gosh, well remembered! It's so we don't forget how many numbers we crossed off. What we do now is put a zero on to our final answer for every number we crossed off. As we crossed off three numbers, we write on three zeros to get a final rough answer of 1,600,000.

## Rough Dividing

There are about 365 days in a year, so here's the sum:

$$365\overline{)6212}$$

As we're dividing, we round both numbers up or both down, so let's round them both up to get

$$400\overline{)7000}$$

Once we have a few zeros in place, the next thing we can do is cross some of them off. Dividing is different from multiplying because *we have to cross off the same number of zeros from both numbers.* Here we'll cross off two zeros each to leave us with:

$$4\overline{)70}$$

No, not with dividing. Right then, we can't make this much simpler so let's hit it...

$$\begin{array}{r} 17 \\ 4\overline{)70} \\ \underline{4\phantom{0}} \\ 30 \\ \underline{28} \\ 2 \end{array}$$

We've got a remainder of 2 but who cares? This is only a rough sum so ignore it and proudly announce your answer...

# OH NO! LOOK...

We've reached the end of the book!

Never mind. Hopefully we'll all meet up again in another *Murderous Maths* book soon, but in the meantime if any sums coming flying at you, you'll be able to whack them back with ribbons round them.

Yes, you'll be just fine so long as you know *the secrets of sums!* You'll never be an expert straight away, but remember, even with kissing, you have to start at the bottom...

# INDEX